# How to Cook Vegetables

# How to Cook

## VEGETABLES

Essential Skills and 90 Foolproof Recipes
(with 270 Variations)

**KIM HOBAN, RDN, CDN, CPT**

ROCKRIDGE
PRESS

Interior and Cover Designer: Emma Hall
Art Producer: Hannah Dickerson
Editor: Anna Pulley
Production Editor: Jenna Dutton

Illustrations © 2020 Tom Bingham

Photography © 2020 Thomas Story, food styling by John Belingheri

ISBN: Print   978-1-64611-558-7
       eBook 978-1-64611-559-4

R0

*To anyone who has yet to discover how*

*delicious Brussels sprouts can be*

# Contents

# Introduction

Vegetables. What comes to mind when you see that word?

*Yuck.*

*Boring.*

*Bland.*

*Do I have to?*

*Eat your veggies or no dessert!*

This book is here to change those negative associations and put an end to the ongoing food fight so many people have with vegetables, the food they know they "should" be eating but don't want to, like to, or even know how to.

I'm a registered dietitian, so it probably doesn't surprise you that vegetables are my jam, but it wasn't always that way. For most of my life, I ate vegetables with a sense of obligation, not enjoyment. My education in nutrition did require some basic food science courses, but I had to learn how to grow, prepare, and cook food on my own. I'm not an expert gardener or a trained chef, but I have been growing vegetables and writing and testing recipes for many years now.

As I learned more about intuitive eating and began honing my own skills in both the garden and the kitchen, I was able to truly appreciate vegetables by focusing on flavor, fun, and satisfaction, not just nutrition. I cringe thinking back to the days when I forced down soggy, plain, steamed vegetables or ate salads with no dressing. If only I had a book like this back then, I would have realized that growing, shopping for, preparing, cooking, and eating vegetables doesn't have to be complicated or tasteless.

My true passion in life is helping people reclaim their love for all foods, veggies included. I want everyone to enjoy vegetables not just because of their health benefits (if you're into that), but because they taste delicious and connect us to the Earth and one another through shared meals, traditions, and culture.

If you're like most people, you probably have some emotional "cabbage" about eating more vegetables. Maybe vegetables have always tasted bland or bitter to you. Perhaps you never learned which veggies are which and even if you can identify them, you don't know what the heck to do with them! With this book, I intend to change all that. When properly prepared, veggies are delicious and fun to add into your meal and snack routine.

In Part 1, we'll start with the basics of getting to know your kitchen and the tools and techniques you'll need to be successful. Part 2 contains in-depth profiles of 30 different vegetables, including their peak season, tips for selecting and storing them, and foods that pair well with them. Part 3 is where we start to have fun in the kitchen with recipes that highlight the variety and vibrance of vegetables. Although many of the recipes in this book are vegetarian, some also include meat and seafood and will be labeled as such.

Once you're armed with the knowledge that vegetables can taste delicious *and* are easy to make, you'll be off to the chopping block. I'm so excited to guide you through this book to help you move from wanting to eat more vegetables, to learning how to select and store them, and finally to preparing delicious vegetable recipes that you'll want to enjoy again and again.

Ready to get started? Then romaine calm and keep an open mind. You're about to bring a little more choy into your life. I'm rooting for you!

# PART ONE

# Getting Started

# CHAPTER 1

# Lettuce Begin: Creating Your Vegetable Kitchen

*To build confidence cooking veggies in the kitchen, you need to learn some basic skills, stock up on tools for success, and have fun along the way. Many cookbooks leave you feeling defeated right from the start with fancy techniques or hard-to-find ingredients, but this one will start with practical tips and tools to inspire creativity in the kitchen.*

## Why Learn to Cook Vegetables?

If you opened this book, I'm guessing you're committed to cooking and eating more vegetables—and for good reason! The dietitian in me is excited to tell you all about the nutritional benefits of veggies, but the perks of plant-forward eating extend well beyond health.

To start, veggies help bulk up meals and add unique textures and flavors. They balance out tougher meats and proteins, as well as chewy grains. We always hear that eating healthy is expensive, but incorporating vegetables can actually save you money, especially when used in conjunction with or in place of animal proteins. Many fresh veggies are inexpensive, especially when in season (more on that shortly), but don't forget about frozen, canned, or jarred versions to save money, cut back on waste, and ensure you're always stocked with vegetables. Prepping and cooking vegetables is also easier than it seems and can be really fun once the creative juices start flowing. Last, but certainly not least, vegetables offer up all kinds of nutritional goodness in the form of essential vitamins, minerals, fiber, and phytochemicals. Eating an assortment of bright and colorful vegetables is associated with a decreased risk of many diseases and improvements in cardiovascular, digestive, and overall health.

While there are thousands of vegetables, in this book we're only covering the most common ones for ease and accessibility. But I promise that there's a veggie to please every cynic! I firmly believe that food should be fun and vegetables can be included in that if you know how to shop for, prepare, and cook them.

## The Benefits of Eating Seasonally

There is no question that vegetables taste better when they are in season. If you've ever enjoyed a fresh summer tomato from the garden, you know this to be true. Beyond taste, eating seasonally can have financial benefits based on simple supply and demand principles. Seasonal eating means you are purchasing vegetables when the supply is highest and therefore the cost is likely lowest. Eating seasonally often means eating locally, which in turn supports the local economy and reduces your carbon footprint. Vegetables are also super nutritious when enjoyed during their peak season, as well as when they are picked ripe, then frozen or otherwise preserved. To help make this even easier, I've included a Seasonal Vegetable Chart (page 203) for a visual reference.

Seasonal eating encourages variety by giving you the chance to experiment with new-to-you veggies and cooking them in different ways. As I hope you'll begin to see from this book and these recipes, roasted broccoli most definitely does not taste the same as raw broccoli florets with dip. You may not like all the options, but you might just like one.

As with most things in life, strive for good, rather than perfect, when it comes to vegetables. The vegetable guide in Part 2 has seasonality information, as will the recipes in Part 3, but keep in mind that eating an off-season vegetable is still better than eating no vegetables at all.

## HOW TO SWAY VEGETABLE NAYSAYERS

Taste matters! If you don't enjoy raw kale or plain broccoli, I don't blame you. Flavor is your friend, so don't be afraid to add fat, herbs, spices, and sauces to veggies to make them taste better. Make vegetables more delicious and enjoyable with the following tips:

**Fat equals flavor.** Butter makes everything better and so does cheese, including vegan versions. Don't worry about "negating" the health benefits of veggies in this way. In fact, oftentimes our bodies need fats to help absorb the nutrients found in veggies.

**Start small.** Find your gateway vegetable and run with it! If you love one tried-and-true veggie, first learn to prepare it in different ways and then slowly branch out to similar vegetables.

**Spice things up.** A little seasoning goes a long way. Kick up the flavor with some spicy sriracha or warm cinnamon flavors. Check out the flavor enhancers (page 9) for more ideas.

**Act like a kid again.** Go into this process with an open mind, letting go of the stories you've told yourself about what you do and don't like. Become a vegetable explorer and add a dip or pair a new vegetable with your favorite food.

## Essential Gear

Kitchen tools and gadgets can be intimidating, not to mention expensive. Work slowly to stock the tools you need for a more functional and fun kitchen. Read on for the basic gear you'll need to succeed, some of which you might already own, plus bonus items that make things easier.

### MUST-HAVES

**Baking dish (9 by 13 inches).** From veg-forward casseroles and baked pastas to roasted veggies, a sturdy baking dish will get a lot of use in your kitchen.

**Cast-iron pan.** Another solid investment, a cast-iron pan will last a lifetime when well cared for. It can transfer right from the stove top to the oven, and it cooks veggies evenly.

**Chef's knife.** This is a nonnegotiable. Your knife doesn't have to be super expensive, but think of a quality knife as a good investment because of how much use it will get.

**Colander.** Metal, plastic, collapsible or not—you decide what works for you, but this tool to rinse and drain veggies is a necessity.

**Cutting board.** A thick wood cutting board will create a stable surface for chopping, though plastic or glass options will also work (and are usually dishwasher-safe, making cleanup easier). If possible, keep separate cutting boards for meats and produce to reduce the risk of cross-contamination and foodborne illness.

**Mason jars.** From shaking up the perfect salad dressing to quick-pickling some vegetables, a glass mason jar is an inexpensive and multifunctional veggie essential.

**Measuring cups and spoons.** It's important to have measuring cups for veggies and other staples, and measuring spoons for spices and herbs. Liquid and dry measures are different, so don't forget a microwave-safe liquid measuring cup.

**Nonstick pan.** No matter what the material, a nonstick pan makes cooking easier and cleanup a breeze.

**Prep bowls.** I love having a few different size bowls in which to put ingredients during prep, to mix recipes, or even to use as a compost/trash bowl for easier cleanup. Look for a set with a few sizes for a variety of uses.

**Sheet pan.** A must-have for baking and roasting, but also for easy-peasy sheet pan meals, such as Sheet Pan Greek Chicken (page 166).

**Spatula.** An inexpensive tool that makes flipping and serving veggies a cinch.

**Stockpot (6 to 8 quarts)/saucepan.** Use these for boiling and steaming, and for one-pot meals, stews, and soups.

**Vegetable peeler.** I prefer a Y-shaped peeler, but a swivel version works just fine.

**Whisk.** For a fast and easy way to create emulsified sauces, dressings, and marinades.

**Tongs.** For tossing and turning veggies with ease or for squeezing fresh citrus over a dish.

**Wooden spoons.** These are gentler on pans than metal, and versatile for stirring, mixing, and serving.

## NICE TO HAVE

**Dutch oven.** A heavy cooking pot used for soups, stews, and braising, a Dutch oven can do the work of a stockpot, slow cooker, deep fryer, and bread maker all in one.

**Food processor.** Use this to chop or shred veggies fast or throw together anything from cauliflower rice to pesto, salsas, and dips.

**Grill pan.** A heavy pan that features raised ridges to offer the flavor and feel of outdoor grilling year-round, even if you don't have access to a grill.

**Immersion blender.** An immersion or hand blender is a good tool for pureeing soups and whipping up smoothies, hummus, salad dressings, and more.

**Kitchen shears.** A good pair of kitchen shears can not only be used to trim herbs, snip artichoke leaves, and separate meat and poultry, but can also be a bottle opener and nut cracker.

**Mandoline.** Even if your knife skills are top-notch, a mandoline can make things easier by creating precise, super-thin cuts in no time.

**Pastry brush.** Use this to coat vegetables with just the right amount of butter, oil, sauces, or dressings.

**Salad spinner.** A colander will do the trick, but a salad spinner is a more efficient way to dry your lettuces, greens, and herbs.

**Skewers.** Available in wood or metal, skewers are long, thin rods that can pierce through veggies for even cooking, or be used to create kebabs.

**Zester.** This flat metal tool with very small holes is used to scrape the outermost skin and oils from lemons and other citrus fruits, adding great flavor to dishes.

## STAY SHARP! HOW TO CARE FOR KNIVES

To make sure your knives are working as they should, and to keep you as safe as possible, it's important to know how to store and sharpen them. No matter what type of knife you're using, a sharp knife is safest. Sharp knives actually help make your veggies taste better, because they ensure a clean, even cut, which means you'll get consistent-size pieces that allow vegetables to roast, sauté, or bake evenly.

Ideally, you should store your knives in a way that helps preserve their sharpness—in a knife block or on a magnetic strip on the wall is best. If your knife must go in a drawer, look for an individual cover to protect the blades from nicks.

How often a knife should be sharpened depends on how often it is used, but because you'll be chopping and dicing regularly with the recipes in this book, you should sharpen your knives a minimum of once a year. A sharpening steel tool, which technically realigns the knife as opposed to sharpening it, should be used before each use. At-home sharpening can be done with a whetstone, a manual or electric knife sharpener, or you can get your knives professionally sharpened.

## Stocking Your Pantry

Now that your drawers and cabinets are stocked with the right gear and gadgets, let's get your pantry set up. Many of these staple items may already be in your kitchen, but if not, add them to the cart on your next grocery store trip.

- Black pepper
- Broth: chicken, vegetable
- Flour and bread crumbs
- Garlic: fresh and powdered
- Honey

- Hot sauce
- Mayonnaise
- Mustard
- Olive oil (regular for cooking, extra-virgin for dressings and cold foods)
- Pasta

- Quinoa
- Rice
- Soy sauce
- Salt
- Vinegar: apple cider, white wine, balsamic

## GO-TO FLAVOR ENHANCERS FOR VEGGIES

**Bacon.** Add smoky and salty notes to veggies by sautéing them in bacon fat or adding bits of bacon on top.

**Butter.** Julia Child is famously quoted as saying, "With enough butter, anything is good." And I tend to agree. If you can, choose a high-quality butter, like Kerrygold Pure Irish Butter for a rich, satisfying flavor.

**Cheese.** My slogan is "Feta makes it betta!" Other popular cheese varieties that complement veggies are cheddar, Parmesan, Gorgonzola, and goat cheese.

**Citrus.** Add a squeeze of fresh lemon, lime, or orange juice to brighten up your dishes.

**Herbs and spices.** Some of my veg-friendly favorites include red pepper flakes, cinnamon, cumin, thyme, rosemary, and basil.

**Nuts, nut butters, and seeds.** To add healthy fats, fiber, and crunch to your veggies, look no further than nuts such as almonds, pecans, and cashews, and seeds like sesame and pumpkin. Nut butters are also great for making sauces and dressings or used as a dip.

# How to Select Veggies

When picking out veggies, always think about the intended use and seasonality. Ask questions, especially if you're purchasing from the farmer who grows the veggies. If that's not an option, use your judgment as well as all your senses. How does a veggie look and feel when you pick it up? Is it bruised or blemished? Is it too firm or overly soft? Does it smell inviting or funky? Are the greens bright and boisterous or dark and wilted? We'll dive into more detail on seasonality and selection tips in Part 2, but for now think about color, texture, weight, and smell when selecting veggies.

**Color.** Brighter is (usually) better.

**Texture.** Feel for smooth and firm veggies. Avoid anything with soft spots, puncture holes, and slimy skins.

**Weight.** Feel the weight of a veggie to make sure it's well hydrated and therefore flavorful.

**Smell.** In general, steer clear of veggies with strong odors, or any odor at all. Many veggies don't smell like much when fresh.

As a last note, please don't automatically skip over ugly veggies. They're just as delicious and nutritious as their perfect-appearing counterparts, and if they're being chopped, pureed, or shredded, it won't matter how uniform or pretty their outsides are!

## ORGANIC VS. CONVENTIONAL

There can be a lot of fear around choosing the "right" produce and shame or guilt when you make decisions between organic versus conventional produce. I'm here to say you can ditch the label and stick with your personal preferences as they relate to taste, price, and seasonality. For example, if a veggie is in season, and the price is the same as or less than the conventional option, go for organic if that feels right for you. But there is certainly no need to buy only organic, and the most important thing (and the reason you snagged this book!) is that you're choosing more vegetables overall. In short, forget the fearmongering around conventional produce and remember that a good wash is what matters most for removing any kind of pesticide and residue.

## How to Store Veggies

The best way to extend the life span of your veggies is to store them properly. For a quick and easy reference, think about how vegetables are stored in the produce section in your grocery store. Asparagus, broccoli, carrots, and celery all go in the refrigerator, as do leafy greens and lettuce. Most root vegetables, potatoes, tomatoes, eggplant, and squash stay on the counter.

In the refrigerator, store lettuces and greens by rinsing, drying, and layering in a tea towel or paper towels in a sealed container or plastic bag. Other veggies can be stored in the crisper drawer or in a separate container in the refrigerator, away from fruits to avoid further ripening.

Be wary of too much moisture, which can lead to faster spoilage, except in the case of asparagus, which can be stored upright in a mason jar filled with water or wrapped in a damp paper towel.

In general, try not to store vegetables for too long, and cook or freeze as much as you can to reduce waste. Keep in mind that high-water vegetables—like cucumber, celery, and lettuces—tend to become soggy or limp when thawed from frozen, so stick to freezing cooked veggies or lower moisture options.

# CHAPTER 2

# Vegetable Prep and Cooking Techniques

*Now that you have a well-stocked pantry and have identified the basic kitchen tools, it's time for the how-to part of the book. This chapter will build your confidence in preparing and cooking vegetables by covering the basics of knife skills and providing foolproof methods for roasting, sautéing, steaming, and more.*

## What Kind of Vegetable Is It?

From root to stem, vegetables can be categorized by what part of the plant they come from. Don't worry, you don't need to memorize which veggies fall into each category, but you can use these groups to better guide you in cleaning, cutting, and prepping any veggie that piques your interest at the grocery store or pops up in your CSA box. Below, I'll break down the most common veggie categories and provide tips and tricks for no-nonsense prep.

### ROOT VEGETABLES

With root vegetables like beets, carrots, potatoes, and parsnips, start by rinsing them well and scrubbing away any dirt and debris. Root veggies can be peeled if you have a vegetable peeler handy, but most can be enjoyed with the skins on as long as they are clean. A good rule of thumb is if you're steaming or pureeing, break out the veggie peeler, but otherwise, save yourself the time and enjoy the benefits of more fiber and nutrition. Start by cutting off the tops and bottoms and with firm, round veggies like potatoes, turnips, and beets, make sure to create a flat edge that will stay put on the cutting board. Then chop them into uniform-size chunks or slice lengthwise for even roasting.

## LEAFY VEGETABLES

It's easy to turn over a new leaf and eat more greens like kale, collards, and Swiss chard when you know how to best prepare them. For most lettuces and greens, rinsing is all the prep you'll need. Start by separating the leaves and washing them in the sink or swishing them in a bowl of cool water to remove any dirt. Don't stress if you don't have a salad spinner; simply transfer to a colander and shake the excess water off before drying them on a clean towel. Pat the leaves dry or roll them up into paper towels for storage, which prevents wilting. For tougher winter greens, tear the leaves away from the stem or stack a few leaves on top of each other and fold in half, running your knife down the rib to speed up the de-ribbing process.

## SEED AND STEM VEGETABLES

Seed and stem veggies, such as cucumber, zucchini, tomatoes, eggplant, and green beans, should all be rinsed clean and dried. The skins are edible, so peeling these vegetables is a personal preference, but be sure to trim any stems or blossoms before chopping. Cucumber, zucchini, squash, and eggplant can be sliced crosswise into circles, or cut in half lengthwise and then chopped into chunks. The size, type, and use of your tomatoes will determine how to prep them. Smaller cherry tomatoes for salads may need no cutting at all, but for larger tomatoes, turn them sideways, slice off the top, and then cut thin slices or dice using a serrated knife.

## STALKS AND TOPS VEGETABLES

Vegetables like celery and leeks or cruciferous veggies like broccoli and cauliflower are grown close to or directly in the ground and should be thoroughly cleaned to remove dirt and grit. For celery, wipe down each stalk with a damp paper towel before removing roots and leaves, and slicing or chopping. I like to prepare leeks by slicing them in half lengthwise and fanning out the stalks, giving them a bath by swishing them around in a bowl of water, and letting the dirt and debris settle at the bottom.

With broccoli and cauliflower, start by removing any outer leaves. Chop broccoli florets away from the stem and for cauliflower, cut around the stalk at an angle before chopping into florets.

## DON'T THROW THAT AWAY!

According to the USDA, food waste is estimated at around 30 to 40 percent of our food supply. We can work to reduce this by utilizing as much of the vegetables as possible.

Salad greens starting to wilt? Bring them back to life with a quick ice bath. And if that doesn't work, use them in a cooked dish instead.

Find yourself tossing broccoli stalks after chopping off the florets? Not so fast! Spiralize the stalks, mash with butter, or chop into a delicious slaw, like the Broccoli-Pear Slaw on page 67.

Use any and all veggie scraps, like potato skins, carrot peels, celery leaves, and mushroom stems to make an easy vegetable broth. Save the scraps as you go. I like to freeze them until I have enough for a batch of broth, and then bring them to a boil with some garlic and herbs, reduce the heat, and simmer for an hour. Voilà—homemade veggie broth!

# How to Wield a Knife

Basic knife skills are essential for cooking up veggies, and the size—of the cut, that is—does matter, as it can influence the cook time, texture, and flavor of a dish. But try not to be intimidated by the terminology. Knife cuts take time to learn, and practice will make perfect, or at least pretty good.

### SLICE

The most basic of knife cuts, slicing is used for roasting, or with veggies that go in salads and on sandwiches. It's the perfect technique for cucumbers, mushrooms, tomatoes, eggplants, and zucchini. A mandoline can be used to make superthin slices, if need be.

### ROUGH CHOP

This is a larger, sometimes uneven cut used on leafy greens, onions, peppers, tomatoes, zucchini, and others. Although there is no official technique for a rough chop, use a knife to chop pieces close in size to one another.

### DICE

This is a smaller, uniform cut that can be various sizes from small (about ¼-inch cubes) to large (¾-inch cubes). Dicing is used for many vegetables, including celery, onions, carrots, peppers, and beets. A large dice works really well for potatoes: Start by creating a flat edge, then cut the potato into slices, then sticks, and then cubes.

### MINCE

Mincing is a very small and not-as-precise chop, most frequently used for herbs and seasoning vegetables, like garlic, onions, and celery.

## JULIENNE

A fancy term for creating matchstick pieces, a julienne cut is most often used in slaws, fries, and sautés, usually using carrots, celery, and potatoes. To make this cut on a carrot, start by peeling the veggie and slicing off the ends. Then trim the sides to make four flat surfaces. Cut lengthwise into rectangles, then rotate the stack 90 degrees to finish off the matchsticks.

# HOW TO BUILD A SHOWSTOPPING SALAD

If the thought of another boring, tasteless salad has you avoiding vegetables altogether, it's time to switch things up. Follow my foolproof method for creating a delicious and satisfying salad, no matter what your personal flavor preferences are.

**Start strong.** Opt for a base of baby spinach, spicy arugula, or hearty kale—or better yet, mix a few types of greens for variety. Not into raw greens? Roasted veggies work, too.

**Add variety.** Tomatoes and cucumbers are salad all-stars, but think outside the box and choose any veggies and fruits you enjoy or have on hand. Bell peppers, artichoke hearts, sliced beets, and butternut squash can all brighten up a bowl of greens.

**Pump things up with protein and fat.** For a truly filling and satisfying salad, turn to beans, chicken, tofu, fish, eggs, or whatever protein floats your boat. Feel fuller longer with fats like avocado, cheese, oil, nuts, and seeds.

**Think about texture *and* flavor.** Top with nuts, seeds, or croutons for added crunch, or dried fruit for a sweet, chewy element.

**Don't skip the dressing.** Think of dressing and condiments as a complement to the flavors already in your bowl. Use a dressing like Easy Herb Vinaigrette (page 96), Italian Dressing (page 99), or Caesar Dressing (page 92) to finish off a vibrant, veggie-filled salad. No more drowning lettuce in dressing to mask unwanted flavors.

Regardless of the type of cut, here's a quick tip for slicing and dicing: When prepping multiple types of veggies, chop from dry to wet (that is, carrots, then onions, then tomatoes) to avoid having to wipe down or rinse off the cutting board each time.

## Cooking Skills that Can't Be Beet

You've sliced and diced; now it's time to turn up the heat and get cooking! The following cooking methods are the most commonly used and can be easily adapted to many vegetable varieties.

### HOW TO ROAST VEGGIES

For perfectly crispy-yet-tender roasted vegetables, set your oven to high heat (400°F to 425°F). Put evenly chopped veggies on a sheet pan with parchment paper or a silicone baking mat (for easier cleanup) and drizzle with olive oil. Or evenly coat them with olive oil by tossing them in a bowl or plastic bag before baking. Roast each veggie separately or try to roast similar types together. Keep in mind that root vegetables take longer (around 45 minutes), cruciferous veggies take around 25 to 30 minutes, and more delicate vegetables like bell peppers, zucchini, and squash can roast faster, in about 15 to 20 minutes.

My biggest tip for roasting is to avoid crowding the pan. Vegetables like a good amount of space to get nice and brown, so spread them evenly and use two pans if you need to. If you can, stir the veggies or shake the pan midway for more even cooking.

You can roast practically any vegetable you'd like, but asparagus, bell peppers, butternut squash, carrots, and cauliflower are a few go-tos if you're just starting out.

### HOW TO SAUTÉ VEGGIES

Sautéing is a method of quickly cooking veggies over high heat with a little bit of fat. Great for getting a veggie side on the table quickly, sautéing works for many vegetables, but particularly for ones that are tender to begin with and need only a short cooking time. Leafy greens, mushrooms, onions, bell peppers, snap peas, and summer squash all lend themselves to sautéing. Start by cutting your veggies uniformly. Then add butter or oil to a sauté pan or skillet, heat it up to coat the pan, and toss the veggies in, stirring occasionally until they are tender with browned surfaces. When sautéing a few types of veggies at once, start with the ones that take longer to cook (think carrots or broccoli) and add in ones that cook faster (like mushrooms) after a few minutes. Season as you cook with salt, pepper, and your favorite herbs and spices.

# HOW TO STEAM, BLANCH, AND BOIL VEGGIES

**Steaming.** Done in just minutes, steaming can save time and produce crisp, bright veggies, if executed properly. Just fill a pot with water up to the bottom of a steamer basket or heat-safe colander. Bring water to a boil, then add veggies and cover. Depending on the size and type of veggie, steaming will take anywhere between 2 and 10 minutes. Thin veggies like asparagus and green beans steam faster than thicker options like carrots or Brussels sprouts. Steaming can even be done in the microwave. Simply put veggies and a little water into a microwave-safe bowl and cover with a microwave-safe plate to seal. Be very careful when removing the plate as the steam can be extremely hot.

**Boiling.** Boiled vegetables may sound gross, but stay with me here, because boiling can be a quick and easy option when done right. Boiling veggies is as simple as pouring chopped vegetables into salted, boiling water. Use only as much water as you need, so as to not lose too much of the nutrients while draining, and cook the veggies only until fork-tender to avoid a mushy, bland mess. Finish boiled veggies by seasoning with preferred spices, herbs, and a drizzle of olive oil or pat of butter.

**Blanching.** This is a good technique if you want to prep and freeze vegetables for later use or simply preserve their bold colors and unique textures. Just have an ice bath (aka a bowl of ice water) ready to go and chop your veggies as you bring water to a boil. Cook to your liking, usually somewhere between 3 and 5 minutes, then immediately transfer cooked veggies to the ice bath. Drain and serve on a crudités platter or freeze for later use in a stir-fry.

## HOW TO BUILD A SUPER VEGETABLE SOUP

Soups are the perfect opportunity to add more veggies into your day or to use up any vegetables that are on the verge of spoiling. Apply the kitchen-sink approach and toss in anything you have on hand. You can't go wrong! Add herbs, spices, and seasonings as well as different proteins and starches/grains to keep things interesting. The combinations for vegetable soups are endless, and the formula for a super soup is simple:

Heat up oil/fat in the pot, cook aromatics first (onion, garlic), then cook the meat (if you're using it), add any and all veggies, and fill the pot with your base (broth or water) and herbs. Bring it all to a boil and then let it simmer. Finish with cream if applicable, puree if desired, garnish with cheese or fresh herbs, and enjoy. In my humble opinion, soup is always best served with a big hunk of delicious, crusty, buttery bread.

## HOW TO QUICK-PICKLE VEGGIES

Pickling vegetables seems pretty fancy and complicated, but can actually be oh-so-easy! Carrots, cucumbers, and radishes probably come to mind right away, but you can pickle pretty much any veggies you have on hand. Personally, I love pickled beets. Look for a seasonal favorite at your local grocery store or farmers' market, preferably crisp veggies like carrots or asparagus for a nice, tangy crunch.

All you need to do is bring a mixture of equal parts vinegar and water to a boil, adding salt and/or sugar and allowing it to dissolve. Pour this brine over veggies stacked in a glass jar. No mason jar? No problem. A heatproof bowl will do just fine; just make sure all the veggies are covered in some brine. Let cool and store covered in the refrigerator for at least 24 hours, allowing veggies to pickle. If you're feeling creative, add some flavor with aromatics like garlic and onion, fresh or dried herbs, and citrus.

Some flavor combos to try:

· Garlic Dill

· Honey Mustard

· Lemon Ginger

# How to Use This Book

Think of this book as your trusty tour guide into the vegetable garden of life. These first few chapters have equipped you with kitchen essentials and basic culinary skills, so now it's time to get down and dirty with 30 of the most common (and a few not so common), versatile veggies. Each vegetable profile will have a short description, tips on selecting, storing, prepping and pairing, plus different varieties to explore. Of course, I'll share a few of my go-to recipes for each veggie, but the possibilities are truly endless once you start exploring the vegetable landscape. The recipes are also outlined in Part 3 and organized by meal type. Each recipe will offer two variations and suggestions for swapping in and out other vegetables, which will hopefully inspire you to get more creative in the kitchen. Though some recipes include meat, many are vegetarian and vegan and will be labeled as such. For peak flavor, nutrition, and cost, recipes will also be labeled by seasonality. You can also refer to the Seasonal Vegetable Chart on page 203 for a quick reference. Keep in mind that when I say "veggie," I'm referring to items commonly found in the produce section of the grocery store. I'm not here to argue about how a tomato is technically a fruit, because we all know we use it like a vegetable.

My hope is that you'll take these recipes and make them your own. When I'm not writing and testing recipes, the truth is I rarely follow them *exactly*. The key ingredients matter, of course, but feel free to take your personal preferences into account, taste as you're cooking, and make tweaks as desired. As you gain inspiration and get more comfortable in the kitchen, you'll be able to create your own veggie-forward fare to enjoy with family and friends.

Ready? Let's broc and roll!

# PART TWO

# The Vegetables

Ready to become a vegetable connoisseur? This comprehensive list of 30 need-to-know veggies features the most widely available varieties and also a few that may be new to you. I couldn't do a deep dive into *every* single vegetable, so you'll notice that some are left out. Avocado (remember, no arguments!), for example, didn't make the cut because I'm willing to bet you don't need another avocado toast recipe. On the other hand, you may be curious about a unique veggie like fiddlehead ferns, but with such a short growing season, we'll leave them for another day (or book). This list was carefully selected with consideration given to the seasonality and availability of fresh veggies, but please don't discount the power of frozen and canned options. Each veggie profile includes tips for shopping, storing, prepping, and cooking, as well as strategies to help you overcome any roadblocks you might face. Finally, and maybe most important, you'll find a few recipe suggestions for each vegetable on the list, so you can put your new veggie cooking skills to work.

# CHAPTER 3

# The Vegetable Profiles

# Artichoke

**Season:** Spring

**About the vegetable:** This green, edible plant is essentially a flower that hasn't bloomed yet, with rough outer leaves and a tender, edible center. Artichokes are native to the Mediterranean region, and thought to be one of the oldest foods in the world.

**How to select:** Look for a deep green color and thick leaves that are tightly closed.

**How to prep:** Rinse well, trim stem and outer leaves.

**How to store:** Keep fresh in the refrigerator for three to five days by trimming the stem and dipping it in water before placing it in an airtight bag.

**Varieties to try:** Globe or French, baby

**Pairs well with:** Butter, spinach, lemon, garlic, Parmesan

**Can easily be swapped with:** Celery, asparagus

**Watch out for:** The spiky thorns on the outer leaves can be intimidating, but start with canned or jarred versions to get a feel for the flavor, and then try steaming a whole artichoke after trimming the stem, crown, and rough outer leaves.

**Recipes:** Creamy Kale-Artichoke Dip (page 71), Greek Grilled Chicken Bowl (page 165), Greek Stuffed Potatoes (page 124), Italian Chopped Salad (page 99), Kale Artichoke Mac and Cheese (page 150), Mediterranean Pizza (page 126), Mediterranean Salad with Crispy Artichokes and Potatoes (page 94), One-Pan Tuscan White Bean Skillet (page 128), Sheet Pan Greek Chicken (page 166), Spinach and Artichoke Mac and Cheese (page 149)

# Asparagus

**Season:** Spring

**About the vegetable:** A green veggie known for its thin edible spears, asparagus gets its name from the Latin and Greek words for "sprout" or "shoot," which is exactly what they do out of the ground.

**How to select:** Look for firm stalks with a bright green color and dry, tightly closed tips. The stalks might even squeak when rubbed together.

**How to prep:** Wash and trim off the woody ends (usually about 1 inch), which can be done by cutting or snapping the spear between your fingers where it bends naturally.

**How to store:** In a mason jar filled with water, or wrapped in a damp towel inside a plastic bag in the crisper drawer in the refrigerator.

**Varieties to try:** White, green, and purple

**Pairs well with:** Lemon, butter, Parmesan, salmon

**Can easily be swapped with:** Green beans

**Watch out for:** The fibrous ends of the stalks are too tough to chew, but they still have nice flavor and can be saved and made into soup.

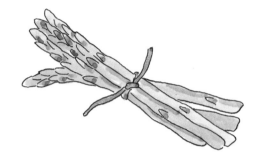

**Recipes:** Asparagus Risotto with Salmon (page 162), Asparagus Soup (page 102), Baked Parmesan Asparagus Fries (page 77), Greek Grilled Chicken Bowl (page 165), Lemon, Asparagus, and Shrimp en Papillote (page 156), Roasted Asparagus with Romesco (page 70), Root-to-Stem Rainbow Salad with Easy Herb Vinaigrette (page 96), Sheet Pan Asparagus, Sweet Potato, and Sausage (page 172), Sheet Pan Greek Chicken (page 166), Simple Sheet Pan Asparagus with Chicken (page 168), Spring Salad with Asparagus and Peas (page 87)

# Beets

**Season:** Late summer, early fall

**About the vegetable:** Often dismissed because of their longer cooking time and a belief that they taste like dirt, beets boast a sweet earthy flavor and plenty of nutrients like folate, fiber, and manganese.

**How to select:** Look for firm, round purple roots with crisp, sturdy green leaves.

**How to prep:** Remove leafy greens to eat or discard, keep the skin on to roast them, then peel and chop, dice, or mash as desired.

**How to store:** Store roots at room temperature for a few days, or keep in the refrigerator for up to 10 days. Beet greens should be removed and used immediately in a salad or cooked into a soup like the Mushroom-Kale Soup with White Beans and Farro (page 105).

**Varieties to try:** Red, golden, orange, striped

**Pairs well with:** Avocado, eggs, goat cheese, other root vegetables, leafy greens, meats

**Can easily be swapped with:** Cabbage, carrots, radish, tomato

**Watch out for:** Red and pink beets can leave stains on hands, cutting boards, and countertops. Use wax paper or gloves when preparing and wrap them in foil when roasting.

**Recipes:** Beet-Berry Sorbet (page 195), Beet Brownie Skillet (page 192), Berry-Beet Smoothie (page 62), Creamy Beet Dip (page 71), Roasted Root Salad (page 98), Root Vegetable Marinara (page 185), Spicy Beet Ketchup (page 190)

# Bell Pepper

**Season:** Summer, early fall

**About the vegetable:** Technically fruits because they contain seeds and are picked from a flowering plant, bell peppers are crispy and mostly sweet. All bell peppers start out green, but yellow, orange, and red varieties are left to ripen longer, and become sweeter (and pricier) as they do so.

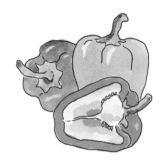

**How to select:** Look for heavy (read: juicy) peppers with a firm stem, and skin that is free from wrinkles, bruises, or dark spots.

**How to prep:** Turn the pepper on its side to slice off the top with the stem and the bottom. Turn the pepper upright, make one slice, then open the pepper flat and use the knife to remove seeds and ribs. Chop up the bottom, and cut around the stem to utilize as much as possible.

**How to store:** In the refrigerator for up to a week

**Varieties to try:** Red, orange, yellow, green, brown, purple

**Pairs well with:** Cheese, eggs, garlic, meat, onions, potatoes, rice, tuna

**Can easily be swapped with:** Poblano, jalapeño (especially if you want to up the spice factor!)

**Watch out for:** The tough outer skin can be hard to cut through, so always chop from the inside out.

**Recipes:** Broccoli and Bell Pepper Stir-Fry with Tempeh (page 125), Crunchy Black Bean and Corn Salad (page 89), Italian Chopped Salad (page 99), Quick Shrimp Pad Thai (page 158), Rainbow Skewers (page 97), Red Pepper Chimichurri (page 183), Simple Ratatouille Soup (page 104), Spaghetti Squash Burrito Bowls (page 121), Spicy Stuffed Sweet Potatoes (page 142), Shakshuka (page 134), Sloppy Joe–Stuffed Peppers (page 139), Tomato and Red Bell Pepper Bruschetta (page 63)

# Bok Choy

**Season:** Winter

**About the vegetable:** Also known as Chinese white cabbage or *pak choi*, bok choy looks like a cross between celery, cabbage, and leafy greens. The stem has a unique crispness and sweet flavor, leading up to tender greens that are delicious steamed, roasted, mixed in a stir-fry, or added to soup.

**How to select:** Pick firm, crisp, white stalks with dark green leaves.

**How to prep:** Remove any damaged or wilted leaves, cut the stalk lengthwise, and submerge it in a bowl of water, swishing around to remove dirt and debris, then drain.

**How to store:** In the crisper drawer in the refrigerator for up to a week

**Varieties to try:** Choy sum, Shanghai, tatsoi

**Pairs well with:** Carrots, garlic, ginger, mushrooms, pork, seafood, soy sauce

**Can easily be swapped with:** Cabbage, celery

**Watch out for:** Cooking times can vary between the thick stalk and tender leaves, so if separating, add the stalks first.

**Recipes:** Bok Choy, Lentil, and Quinoa Bowls with Quick-Pickled Radishes (page 114), Bok Choy Noodle Bowl (page 115), Carrot and Bok Choy Sauté (page 78), Mushroom, Bok Choy, and Shrimp Stir-Fry (page 157), Salmon Cakes with Bok Choy Slaw (page 161), Shrimp Stir-Fry with Bok Choy and Broccoli (page 157)

# Broccoli

**Season:** Late fall, winter, early spring

**About the vegetable:** One of the more popular cruciferous veggies, these beautiful little trees are packed full of vitamin C, fiber, and calcium.

**How to select:** Look for large, tightly packed green heads, thick stalks, and no yellowing or discoloration.

**How to prep:** Cut off the tough dry end of the stalk, then chop florets off from the stem up. Peel or trim away the outer stalk and cut to use as well.

**How to store:** Store cold in the refrigerator in a produce bag for up to a week

**Varieties to try:** Broccoli rabe, Romanesco, broccolini

**Pairs well with:** Butter, cheese, citrus fruits, eggs, garlic, onions, soy sauce, yogurt

**Can easily be swapped with:** Cauliflower

**Watch out for:** Overcooking broccoli leads to mushy and brown florets. Cook them for a short time at a high cooking temperature until just tender.

**Recipes:** Broccoli and Pea Shrimp Stir-Fry (page 157), Broccoli-Basil Pesto (page 182), Broccoli and Bell Pepper Stir-Fry with Tempeh (page 125), Broccoli and Black Bean Tacos (page 113), Broccoli Calzones (page 148), Broccoli-Cheddar Stuffed Potatoes (page 123), Broccoli Chicken Fried Rice (page 164), Broccoli Crust Pizza (page 119), Broccoli, Lemon, and White Bean Pasta (page 120), Broccoli and Lentil Quinoa Bowl (page 115), Broccoli-Pear Slaw (page 67), Broccoli Sage Tortellini (page 151), Pesto Broccoli Chicken (page 167), Roasted Broccoli Tacos with Garlicky Black Bean Spread (page 133), Salmon Cakes with Broccoli-Pear Slaw (page 161), Shrimp Stir-Fry with Bok Choy and Broccoli (page 157), Veggie-Loaded Potato Soup with Bacon (page 106)

# Brussels Sprouts

**Season:** Fall and winter

**About the vegetable:** Brussels sprouts originated in Belgium, hence their name. Part of the cruciferous vegetable family, Brussels sprouts look like mini cabbages but actually grow on long stalks, which are becoming more widely available at farmers' markets and grocery stores. If you can, pick these because your Brussels sprouts will be even fresher.

**How to select:** Look for nice green bulbs with tight leaves, and no signs of yellowing or black spots.

**How to prep:** Wash with cold water, using a colander to drain, peel away loose wilted leaves, and cut off the small stem.

**How to store:** In the refrigerator in a plastic bag for up to a week

**Varieties to try:** Dagan, diablo, Long Island, Rubine

**Pairs well with:** Bacon, basil, beans, butter, garlic, ginger, mustard, nuts, olive oil, onion

**Can easily be swapped with:** Broccoli, cabbage

**Watch out for:** Keep in mind that the smaller the sprout, the sweeter and more tender it will be.

**Recipes:** Autumn Roasted Vegetable Wraps (page 111), Balsamic Brussels Sprout Stir-Fry (page 125), Balsamic Maple Brussels Sprouts (page 75), Brussels Sprout Pesto (page 182), Honey-Sriracha Brussels Sprouts (page 75), Mini Brussels and Bacon Bites (page 65), Roasted Brussels Sprout Tacos with Garlicky Black Bean Spread (page 132), Roasted Vegetable Salad with Goat Cheese (page 98), Sweet Sprout Slaw (page 67)

# Cabbage

**Season:** Late fall, winter

**About the vegetable:** Best known as the feature ingredient in coleslaw and sauerkraut, cabbage can be blanched, boiled, steamed, stuffed, and, of course, enjoyed raw.

**How to select:** Keep an eye out for firm cabbages with crisp, closed leaves, showing no signs of wilting or damage.

**How to prep:** Peel away tough outer leaves and wash well under running water before chopping.

**How to store:** Most cabbage varieties can be kept in a plastic bag in the refrigerator for up to two weeks, while napa cabbage will only stay fresh for a few days.

**Varieties to try:** Green, napa, red, savoy

**Pairs well with:** Apples, beef, ginger, mushrooms, pork, vinegar

**Can easily be swapped with:** Broccoli, Brussels sprouts, kale

**Watch out for:** When cooking red cabbage, it can fade to purple or blue, so pair it with an acid (lemon or vinegar) to keep its color.

**Recipes:** Apple, Cheddar, and Collard Wraps (page 110), Apple, Cheddar, and Spinach Salad (page 111), Foil-Wrapped Braised Cabbage (page 73), Homemade Sauerkraut (page 188), Salmon Cakes over Sesame-Ginger Slaw (page 160), Spiced Cauliflower and Chickpea Tacos (page 112)

# Carrots

**Season:** Spring, summer, fall, winter

**About the vegetable:** Though modern-day carrots are typically orange, centuries ago, white, purple, and yellow varieties were the norm. Packed with vitamin A, carrots are certainly good for your eyes, but these sweet, crunchy roots have other health benefits, such as improved digestive health, stronger immunity, and reduced risk of heart disease.

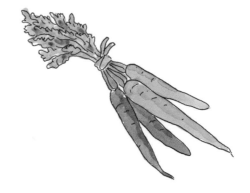

**How to select:** Look for evenly colored roots that don't look too wet or too dry. If the tops are still attached, they should look green and lively, not wilted.

**How to prep:** Wash and scrub with a vegetable brush to remove dirt, leave whole, or chop as needed. Enjoy them raw or cooked.

**How to store:** Remove the green tops and keep the carrots in the refrigerator for up to two weeks, stored in an open produce bag.

**Varieties to try:** Orange, white, yellow, purple

**Pairs well with:** Beef, celery, chicken, onions, peas, potatoes

**Can easily be swapped with:** Parsnips, squash, turnips, zucchini

**Watch out for:** White coating (or "blush") can appear on carrots that are starting to dry out. They're still safe to eat and can be rehydrated in a quick cold-water bath.

**Recipes:** Carrot and Bok Choy Sauté (page 78), Carrot Cake Cookies (page 201), Carrot Fries (page 68), Carrot-Mango Sorbet (page 195), Carrot, Green Bean, and Tempeh Peanut Stir-Fry (page 125), Cauliflower and Root Vegetable Mash Bowls with Ground Beef (page 178), Chicken Fried Rice (page 163), Creamy Kale-Artichoke Dip (page 71), Green Bean and Carrot Sauté (page 78), Lemony Leeks and Carrots with Parmesan (page 117), Lentil Bolognese over Spaghetti (page 138), Quick Shrimp Pad Thai (page 158), Roasted Vegetable Salad with Goat Cheese (page 98), Root Vegetable Marinara (page 185), Root-to-Stem Rainbow Salad with Easy Herb Vinaigrette (page 96), Salmon Cakes over Sesame-Ginger Slaw (page 160), Shepherd's Pie–Stuffed Sweet Potatoes (page 141), Simple Fermented Carrots (page 189), Simple Kachumber Salad (page 84), Sloppy Joe–Stuffed Peppers (page 139), Snow Pea and Carrot Sauté (page 78), Summer Slaw with Zucchini and Carrots (page 67), Sweet Potato and Root Vegetable Mash (page 79), Tuna Collard Wraps (page 159), Veggie-Loaded Potato Soup with Bacon (page 106)

# Cauliflower

**Season:** Fall and winter

**About the vegetable:** The shapeshifter of the vegetable world, cauliflower is a cruciferous veggie that is gaining popularity as a substitute for mashed potatoes, rice, pasta, and even pizza crust (page 118).

**How to select:** The best cauliflower heads feel firm with tightly packed florets and will be free of discoloration or bruising.

**How to prep:** Remove the outer leaves, turn cauliflower over, and cut around the stalk at an angle before chopping into florets.

**How to store it:** Store up to a week, head down in the crisper drawer in the refrigerator, to prevent moisture from accumulating.

**Varieties to try:** White, purple, yellow, green

**Pairs well with:** Beans, butter, cheese, onions, potatoes, thyme, tomatoes

**Can easily be swapped with:** Broccoli, cabbage

**Watch out for:** Strong-smelling cauliflower may be starting to turn, meaning the taste will be off, too.

**Recipes:** Cauliflower and Root Vegetable Mash Bowls with Ground Beef (page 178), Cauliflower Crust Pizza (page 118), Cauliflower Potato Soup with Bacon (page 107), Cauliflower Steaks with Romesco Sauce (page 69), Root-to-Stem Rainbow Salad with Easy Herb Vinaigrette (page 96), Spiced Cauliflower and Chickpea Enchiladas (page 113), Spiced Cauliflower and Chickpea Tacos (page 112), Spinach Pesto Cauliflower Crust Pizza (page 119), Sweet and Spicy Cauliflower (page 75)

# Celery

**Season:** Spring, summer, fall, winter; best mid-to-late summer

**About the vegetable:** One of the most well-known vegetables and used in everything from soups to kids' snacks, celery is crunchy with a mild but refreshing flavor.

**How to select:** Look for firm, crisp stalks and pay close attention to the leaves, making sure they are not limp, wilted, or yellowing.

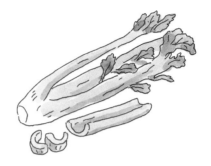

**How to prep:** Cut off the leaves and base, then chop or slice to desired size.

**How to store:** Keep in a perforated bag or wrapped in a damp towel in the crisper drawer of the refrigerator for up to two weeks.

**Varieties to try:** Celeriac (root)

**Pairs well with:** Carrots, cheese, cream cheese, grains, lentils, nut butters, onions, potatoes

**Can easily be swapped with:** Asparagus, bok choy, fennel, jicama

**Watch out for:** The strings in celery ribs can be a texture turn off for some, so use a vegetable peeler to quickly and easily remove the outer strings.

**Recipes:** Braised Mediterranean-Style Celery (page 117), Celery Soup (page 101), Fall Spinach Salad (page 88), Lemony Lentil-Turnip Soup (page 103), Lentil Bolognese over Spaghetti (page 138), Mushroom-Kale Soup with White Beans and Farro (page 105), Shepherd's Pie–Stuffed Sweet Potatoes (page 141), Summer Squash Soup (page 102), Tuna Collard Wraps (page 159)

# Corn

**Season:** Summer

**About the vegetable:** Nothing beats corn on the cob in the summer, and contrary to popular belief, it is rich in nutrients like B vitamins and potassium. Fun fact: There is one silk for every kernel of corn on each cob.

**How to select:** For the best fresh corn, look for tightly wrapped, bright-green husks with brown tassels, and feel for firm kernels. Some say it's against corn etiquette to peel back the husk and look before buying, but I think it's okay to take a tiny peek.

**How to prep:** Husk the corn by peeling back the leaves and silk, then cutting off the ends. If taking the kernels off the cob, lay it flat and slice one side completely off to create a stable base to remove the rest.

**How to store:** Keep the husk on and store in a tightly wrapped bag in the refrigerator for up to three days to keep the corn from drying out.

**Varieties to try:** White, yellow, bicolor, multicolor

**Pairs well with:** Beef, butter, chicken, chili powder, cilantro, fish, peppers, salt, tomatoes

**Can easily be swapped with:** Peas

**Watch out for:** To make husking easier, slice the end of the cob and microwave for about one minute, after which the husks should slide right off.

**Recipes:** Black Bean and Corn Salad (page 89), Crunchy Black Bean and Corn Salad (page 89), Lemony Turnip-Corn Soup (page 103), Roasted Corn and Tomato Tacos with Black Bean Spread (page 133), Root-to-Stem Rainbow Salad with Easy Herb Vinaigrette (page 96), Southwest Sweet Potato Pizza (page 126), Spaghetti Squash Burrito Bowls (page 121), Spicy Stuffed Sweet Potatoes (page 142), Summer Grilled Vegetable Salad (page 98), Sweet Potato Sheet Pan Nachos (page 145), Tex-Mex Chicken Bowl (page 166)

# Cucumbers

**Season:** Summer

**About the vegetable:** One of the many vegetables that is technically a fruit, cucumbers are a favorite for their calming, light scent, refreshing taste, and juicy texture.

**How to select:** Pick out long, firm, green cucumbers with no soft spots or discoloration.

**How to prep:** Peel if the skin is tough, or leave it on and halve, slice, or chop as desired.

**How to store:** Loosely wrap in plastic or with paper towels in a plastic bag, and keep in the refrigerator for up to a week.

**Varieties to try:** Armenian, English, garden, kirby, lemon, Persian

**Pairs well with:** Basil, cheese, citrus, dill, seafood, tomato, yogurt

**Can easily be swapped with:** Celery, jicama, zucchini

**Watch out for:** Most seeds are edible, but they can also be scooped out to stuff cucumbers, or enjoy as seedless snacks.

**Recipes:** Cooled Cucumber-Avocado Soup (page 101), Creamy Cucumber-Onion Salad (page 84), Cucumber Ice Cream (page 200), Cucumber Mojito Sorbet (page 195), Greek Bruschetta (page 64), Greek Salad Skewers (page 91), Simple Kachumber Salad (page 84), Sweet Cucumber Salad with Toasted Sesame Oil (page 84), Tzatziki (page 191), Watermelon-Jicama Salad (page 86), Watermelon, Tomato, and Cucumber Salad (page 86)

# Eggplant

**Season:** Summer and early fall

**About the vegetable:** Another veggie that is technically a fruit, eggplant is also a nightshade and closely related to potatoes and tomatoes.

**How to select:** Look for smooth, firm, and glossy skin.

**How to prep:** Cut off the stem, leaves, and end. If the skin is thick, peel to remove.

**How to store:** Keep in a loosely wrapped plastic bag in the refrigerator for up to a week.

**Varieties to try:** Chinese, globe, Indian, Italian, Japanese, Sicilian, white

**Pairs well with:** Bell peppers, cheese, garlic, olive oil, potatoes, tomatoes

**Can easily be swapped with:** Turnip, rutabaga, zucchini

**Watch out for:** Salting eggplant prior to cooking will reduce the moisture and bitterness. Sprinkle salt on the cut eggplant and let sit for 30 minutes, if you can, or salt and microwave for about 5 minutes to dry it out.

**Recipes:** Baba Ghanoush (page 71), Crispy Eggplant Bites (page 72), Moussaka-Stuffed Eggplant (page 175), Roasted Vegetable Ratatouille Soup (page 104), Simple Ratatouille Soup (page 104), Stuffed Eggplant Parm (page 176), Stuffed Portobello Mushrooms Layered with Eggplant (page 130), Tex-Mex Stuffed Eggplant (page 176)

# Green Beans

**Season:** Spring, summer

**About the vegetable:** Think beyond mushy casseroles and enjoy green beans in a variety of ways, raw or cooked. As their name indicates, they are typically green, but might also show up in yellow or purple versions.

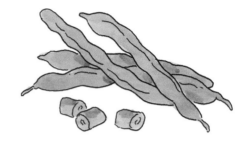

**How to select:** Select intact pods with a bright color.

**How to prep:** Wash and trim or snap off the stem ends before cutting or cooking.

**How to store it:** Keep in a tightly closed bag in the refrigerator for up to five days.

**Varieties to try:** Pole, bush

**Pairs well with:** Bacon, basil, butter, cheese, chicken, lemon, mushrooms, olive oil, onions, pork, potatoes, red pepper flakes, tomatoes, vinegar

**Can easily be swapped with:** Asparagus, peas

**Watch out for:** Be careful not to trim off too much of the stem ends so that the beans don't absorb extra water when cooking.

**Recipes:** Carrot, Green Bean, and Tempeh Peanut Stir-Fry (page 125), Garlicky Green Beans (page 74), Green Bean and Carrot Sauté (page 78), Grilled Green Beans, Mushrooms, and Potatoes (page 172), Mediterranean Green Bean Salad (page 95), Pumpkin-Tofu Curry with Green Beans (page 137), Sheet Pan Green Beans, Carrots, and Chicken (page 168), Sheet Pan Sausage, Green Beans, Mushrooms, and Potatoes (page 171), Spicy Sweet Potato Curry with Green Beans (page 137), Spring Salad with Asparagus and Peas (page 87)

# Jicama

**Season:** Fall

**About the vegetable:** Also known as Mexican yam bean or Mexican turnip, jicama is a brown root vegetable with a crispy and sweet inside. Raw jicama is perfect for snacking and in salads and slaws.

**How to select:** Choose medium-size, firm, and unblemished tubers that feel heavy.

**How to prep:** Peel, chop, or shred, and enjoy raw or cooked.

**How to store:** Keep uncovered in a dark, cool place, or in the refrigerator for several weeks. If partially chopped, cover the cut side with plastic wrap and keep in the refrigerator.

**Varieties to try:** Jicama de agua, jicama de leche

**Pairs well with:** Avocado, cilantro, citrus fruit, chiles, cucumber, jalapeño, mango, onion

**Can easily be swapped with:** Radish, water chestnut

**Watch out for:** The tough skin needs to be peeled, but it may be worth using a paring knife over a vegetable peeler for a safe and efficient job.

**Recipes:** Cinnamon Jicama Chips (page 196), Jicama Churros (page 196), Jicama Pico de Gallo (page 186), Watermelon-Jicama Salad (page 86), Watermelon-Jicama Skewers (page 86)

# Leeks

**Season:** Spring

**About the vegetable:** A member of the *allium* genus, leeks are sweeter with a more delicate flavor than its onion and shallot relatives. One cup of leeks contains almost half the recommended daily value of vitamin K, plus they are a good source of vitamin B6, folate, and manganese.

**How to select:** Aim for crisp and clean-looking stalks with bright green leaves and the roots still attached. (The roots look like a fringe.)

**How to prep:** Slice in half lengthwise, and rinse very well to remove dirt between layers. I like to give them a bath and fan out the stalks, swishing them around in a bowl of water.

**How to store:** Untrimmed and unwashed in a loose plastic bag in the refrigerator for a week, sometimes up to two.

**Varieties to try:** Early season (smaller), late season (thicker stalks, stronger flavor)

**Pairs well with:** Butter, carrots, cheese, fish, meat, potatoes, rice

**Can easily be swapped with:** Scallions, onions, shallots

**Watch out for:** The tough green ends of the leek leaves usually get discarded but can be used to add extra flavor to soups and stews. Skim them out before serving, or put the tops in a cheesecloth while cooking.

**Recipes:** Braised Mediterranean-Style Leeks (page 116), Lemony Leeks and Carrots with Parmesan (page 117), Lovely Leeks with Garlic (page 74), One-Pan Lemony Leek Risotto with Salmon (page 153), Veggie-Loaded Potato Soup with Bacon (page 106)

# Lettuces

**Season:** Spring, summer, fall, winter

**About the vegetable:** Best known as a base for salads, lettuce can also be used as wraps, in sandwiches, and in cooked meals. With a wide range of colors, flavors, and textures, lettuces offer a good source of vitamins A, C, and K, and fiber.

**How to select:** Choose fresh, crisp-looking leaves with no signs of wilting or damage.

**How to prep:** Wash leaves by separating and submerging them in cold water, shake to dry, and use a salad spinner or lay out on towels to dry before storing.

**How to store:** Wrap with a dry paper towel and store in an airtight bag in the refrigerator for up to a week.

**Varieties to try:** Arugula, Bibb, Boston, endive, green leaf, iceberg, red leaf, romaine

**Pairs well with:** Avocado, berries, carrots, cheese, cucumbers, mustard, olive oil, peppers, tomatoes, vinegar

**Can easily be swapped with:** Collards, kale, Swiss chard

**Watch out for:** Bruising and wilting can occur easily with sensitive greens, so be gentle. Store lettuce on top of other veggies, and keep it away from fruits like apples and pears that can contribute to ripening and wilting.

**Recipes:** Endive-Walnut Salad (page 90), Greek Salad Skewers (page 91), Grilled Romaine Caesar Salad (page 92), Italian Chopped Salad (page 99), Root-to-Stem Rainbow Salad with Easy Herb Vinaigrette (page 96), Spring Salad with Asparagus and Peas (page 87), Sweet and Spicy Citrus Salad (page 85)

# Mushrooms

**Season:** Fall and winter

**About the vegetable:** Known as the "meat" of the vegetable world, these "fun guys" (fungi) are packed with B vitamins, potassium, selenium, fiber, and more.

**How to select:** Pick firm mushrooms that are not slimy.

**How to prep:** Clean just before cooking by wiping with a damp paper towel, remove stems if necessary, and slice as desired. Avoid soaking in water or rinsing too much, because mushrooms can absorb excess water and lose flavor.

**How to store:** Keep for up to a week in the refrigerator in a brown paper bag.

**Varieties to try:** Cremini, portobello, white button, shiitake, oyster, chanterelle, porcini, morel

**Pairs well with:** Basil, beef, chicken, onions, tomatoes

**Can easily be swapped with:** Not easy to swap, but try eggplant or zucchini

**Watch out for:** Overcrowding the pan with mushrooms can lead to steaming instead of sautéing, so give the shrooms room.

**Recipes:** Bok Choy, Lentil, and Quinoa Bowls with Quick-Pickled Radishes (page 114), Brussels Sprout Pesto Portobello Burgers (page 131), Crispy Mushrooms (page 72), Grilled Green Beans, Mushrooms, and Potatoes (page 172), Lasagna-Style Stuffed Portobello Mushrooms (page 129), Lentil Mushroom Bolognese (page 138), Mushroom and Pea Risotto (page 162), Mushroom, Bok Choy, and Shrimp Stir-Fry (page 157), Mushroom-Kale Soup with White Beans and Farro (page 105), Mushroom Marinara (page 185), Pesto Portobello Burgers (page 131), Pesto Provolone Portobello Pizza (page 131), Sheet Pan Sausage, Green Beans, Mushrooms, and Potatoes (page 171), Sloppy Joe–Stuffed Peppers (page 139), Stuffed Portobello Mushrooms Layered with Eggplant (page 130), Sweet Potato–Mushroom Burgers (page 144), Tortellini with Mushroom Bolognese (page 151), Tortellini with Mushrooms and Sage (page 151)

# Peas

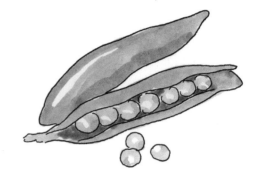

**Season:** Spring, winter

**About the Vegetable:** These small but mighty green veggies are actually legumes and add a touch of natural sweetness to dishes. Frozen peas do double duty by serving as an ice pack in times of need, but otherwise use them to boost the nutrition of soups, pasta dishes, and more.

**How to select:** Look for fresh-looking, firm pods with an even, green color.

**How to prep:** Wash, dry, snap or pop off the stem, and peel away the string down the center of the pod. Open and pour the peas into a bowl.

**How to store:** Keep in a plastic bag in the crisper drawer of the refrigerator for two to three days.

**Varieties to try:** English, garden, green, snow, sugar snap

**Pairs well with:** Asparagus, butter, cheese, chicken, dill, grains, mint, olive oil, onions, pasta

**Can easily be swapped with:** Broccoli, corn, green beans

**Watch out for:** The pods of snow and sugar snap varieties are edible and can be left intact for cooking.

**Recipes:** Broccoli and Pea Shrimp Stir-Fry (page 157), Chicken Fried Rice (page 163), Cod en Papillote (page 156), Green Pea Guacamole (page 184), Mushroom and Pea Risotto (page 162), Pasta with Peas and Bacon (page 173), Shrimp Pad Thai with Snow Peas (page 158), Snow Pea and Carrot Sauté (page 78), Spring Salad with Asparagus and Peas (page 87)

# Pumpkins

**Season:** Fall

**About the vegetable:** Oh gourd, pumpkins are the most celebrated fall vegetable, and for good reason. Thinking beyond the infamous pumpkin spice latte, pumpkin works well in everything from breakfast to dessert, and it elicits a sense of nostalgia, coziness, and comfort.

**How to select:** For carving and decorating, bigger pumpkins are great. For cooking, look for small to medium-size orange pumpkins with a sturdy and dry brown stem, and no bruises or soft spots.

**How to prep:** To roast, either remove the stem and scoop out the seeds and strings, or slice the pumpkin in half and scoop the innards from each side.

**How to store:** Keep in a cool, but not cold, location for one to two months.

**Varieties to try:** Cheese, Cinderella, sugar

**Pairs well with:** Brown sugar, cayenne, cinnamon, cloves, ginger, milk, nutmeg, oats, rice, vanilla

**Can easily be swapped with:** Sweet potato, winter squash

**Watch out for:** Although the stringy insides of pumpkin are inedible, you can enjoy the seeds raw, or rinse, dry, and roast them at 350°F on an oiled sheet pan for 20 to 25 minutes.

**Recipes:** Pumpkin, Fig, and Apple Crisp (page 197), Pumpkin Power Smoothie (page 62), Pumpkin-Tofu Curry with Green Beans (page 137), Pumpkin-Zucchini Crisp (page 198), Sweet Potato–Pumpkin Mash (page 79)

# Radishes

**Season:** Spring

**About the vegetable:** This member of the mustard family is known for being crunchy and sweet, but also peppery.

**How to select:** Look for bright-colored bulbs that are firm. If the leaves are attached, make sure those are also vibrant and not wilted.

**How to prep:** Wash, trim ends and any excess roots, and slice, dice, grate, or enjoy whole.

**How to store:** Remove the leaves before keeping radish roots in a bag in the refrigerator for up to a week.

**Varieties to try:** Black, cherry belle, daikon, watermelon

**Pairs well with:** Asparagus, cucumber, grains, olive oil

**Can easily be swapped with:** Celery, English cucumber

**Watch out for:** The most peppery part of a radish is the skin, so peel it to tone down the taste.

**Recipes:** Bok Choy, Lentil, and Quinoa Bowls with Quick-Pickled Radishes (page 114), Cucumber-Radish Salsa (page 186), Garlic Sliced Radishes (page 189), Radish Tzatziki (page 191), Sweet and Spicy Citrus Salad (page 85), Zucchini-Radish Salsa (page 186)

# Rutabaga

**Season:** Spring, fall, winter

**About the vegetable:** This often-overlooked root veggie is a mix between a cabbage and a turnip, but it tastes sweet and can be prepared just like potatoes or sweet potatoes. Rutabagas are high in beta carotene and are golden yellow in color as a result.

**How to select:** Opt for a heavy and firm rutabaga with smooth skin.

**How to prep:** Trim off the ends and peel away the waxy skin using a paring knife.

**How to store:** Keep in the refrigerator or in a cool, dark place for a few weeks or even months.

**Varieties to try:** American purple top, Joan, Laurentian, magres

**Pairs well with:** Butter, fruits, garlic, meat, milk, other root vegetables

**Can easily be swapped with:** Carrots, turnips, potatoes, sweet potatoes

**Watch out for:** Many store-bought rutabagas are coated with wax, so be sure to wash well, scrub, and/or peel the skin before eating.

**Recipes:** Italian Rutabaga Fries (page 68), Roasted Vegetable Salad with Goat Cheese (page 98), Rutabaga Fries (page 68)

# Spinach

**Season:** Spring

**About the vegetable:** The most versatile leafy green vegetable, spinach can be used in smoothies, salads, baked goods, cooked entrées, and sides.

**How to select:** Choose dark green, crisp-looking leaves with no signs of wilting.

**How to prep:** Wash and remove any tough stems, then enjoy raw, or chop, slice, or tear leaves, depending on how you'll be cooking it.

**How to store:** Loosely wrap in a paper towel and store in a bag in the refrigerator for up to five days.

**Varieties to try:** Flat-leaf, savoy, semi-savoy

**Pairs well with:** Avocado, bacon, eggs, fruit, mushrooms, nuts, seafood, soft cheeses, tomatoes

**Can easily be swapped with:** Arugula, bok choy, kale, Swiss chard

**Watch out for:** Spinach reduces significantly when cooked, so always buy more than you think you will need to serve.

**Recipes:** Apple, Cheddar, and Spinach Salad (page 111), Breakfast Spinach-Feta Calzones (page 148), Broccoli, Lemon, and White Bean Pasta (page 120), Chimichurri (page 183), Fall Spinach Salad (page 88), Green Shakshuka (page 135), Lasagna-Style Stuffed Portobello Mushrooms (page 129), Ricotta-Spinach Calzones (page 147), Root-to-Stem Rainbow Salad with Easy Herb Vinaigrette (page 96), Spaghetti Spinach Parmesan (page 174), Spinach and Artichoke Mac and Cheese (page 149), Spinach and White Bean Stuffed Spaghetti Squash (page 122), Spinach-Kale Pesto (page 182), Spinach Pesto Cauliflower Crust Pizza (page 119), Strawberry, Spinach, and Cucumber Salad (page 88), Summer Grilled Vegetable Salad (page 98), Super Green Guacamole (page 184), Sweet Potato–Spinach Frittata (page 127)

# Sweet Potato

**Season:** Fall, winter

**About the vegetable:** Elongated tubers with tapered ends, sweet potatoes can have orange, purple, or white flesh, and all are delicious well beyond sweet potato casserole.

**How to select:** To ensure sweetness and easier prep, seek out small to medium-size sweet potatoes that are smooth and firm. Avoid any with extra thin stringy roots, as they may be getting old and tough.

**How to prep:** Scrub well and cook whole (with or without skin), or chop into cubes, wedges, or fries.

**How to store:** Keep in a cool, dark place for several weeks. Once cooked, store in the refrigerator for up to five days.

**Varieties to try:** Beauregard, garnet, Hannah, Japanese, jewel, Okinawa, purple stokes

**Pairs well with:** Beans, butter, brown sugar, cream, cinnamon, ginger, maple syrup, nuts

**Can easily be swapped with:** Potatoes, butternut squash

**Watch out for:** To prevent over-drying sweet potatoes that you have chopped for a later meal, store them in the refrigerator in cold water.

**Recipes:** Fall Harvest Pizza (page 126), Root Vegetable Marinara (page 185), Sheet Pan Asparagus, Sweet Potato, and Sausage (page 172), Shepherd's Pie–Stuffed Sweet Potatoes (page 141), Southwest Sweet Potato Pizza (page 126), Spicy Stuffed Sweet Potatoes (page 142), Spicy Sweet Potato Curry with Green Beans (page 137), Squash and Sweet Potato Mash (page 79), Sweet Potato Brownies (page 193), Sweet Potato Burgers (page 143), Sweet Potato Chips (page 196), Sweet Potato Cookies (page 201), Sweet Potato Ice Cream (page 200), Sweet Potato–Kale Frittata (page 127), Sweet Potato–Mushroom Burgers (page 144), Sweet Potato–Pumpkin Mash (page 79), Sweet Potato and Root Vegetable Mash (page 79), Sweet Potato–Spinach Frittata (page 127), Veggie-Loaded Sweet Potato Fries (page 146)

# Tomatoes

**Season:** Summer

**About the vegetable:** Though technically a fruit, nutritionally speaking, the tomato is considered to be a vegetable and comes in a variety of shapes, sizes, and colors. If tomatoes aren't in season or local, you'll actually want to choose canned versions for cooking, because they are picked and processed at the peak of freshness.

**How to select:** Choose smooth, firm tomatoes with shiny skin and no visible bruising or cuts. If you can, smell the stem. A strong, fresh aroma means a ripe, delicious tomato.

**How to prep:** Remove the stems and use a sharp, serrated knife to cut. If removing the seeds for a recipe, simply slice the tomato in half and squeeze lightly over a bowl to remove seeds and excess juices.

**How to store:** At room temperature, but if they're fully ripe and you aren't going to eat them right away, you *can* chill tomatoes in the refrigerator for a few days.

**Varieties to try:** Beefsteak, cherry, grape, heirloom, plum

**Pairs well with:** Basil, cucumbers, eggs, feta, mozzarella, mushrooms, olives, pasta

**Can easily be swapped with:** Cucumbers, peppers

**Watch out for:** Aluminum cookware is not compatible with the acid in tomatoes, because it makes them taste bitter.

**Recipes:** Black Bean and Corn Salad (page 89), BLT Bites (page 65), Cucumber-Radish Salsa (page 186), Greek Salad Skewers (page 91), Green Pea Guacamole (page 184), Grilled Romaine Cobb Salad (page 93), Italian Chopped Salad (page 99), Italian Salad Skewers (page 99), Lentil Bolognese over Spaghetti (page 138), Mediterranean Pizza (page 126), Mediterranean Salad with Crispy Artichokes and Potatoes (page 94), Moussaka-Stuffed Eggplant (page 175), Mushroom Marinara (page 185), One-Pan Tuscan White Bean Skillet (page 128), Pesto Portobello Burgers (page 131), Pesto Tomato Mozzarella Chicken (page 167), Rainbow Skewers (page 97), Ratatouille Salad (page 104), Roasted Corn and Tomato Tacos with Black Bean Spread (page 133), Roasted Vegetable Ketchup (page 190), Romesco Sauce (page 187), Root Vegetable Marinara (page 185), Root-to-Stem Rainbow Salad with Easy Herb Vinaigrette (page 96), Shakshuka (page 134), Shepherd's Pie–Stuffed Sweet Potatoes (page 141), Simple Kachumber Salad (page 84), Simple Marinara Sauce (page 185), Simple Ratatouille Soup (page 104), Sloppy Joe–Stuffed Peppers (page 139), Sloppy Joe–Stuffed Tomatoes (page 140), Southwest Sweet Potato Pizza (page 126), Spaghetti Squash Burrito Bowls (page 121), Spring Salad with Asparagus and Peas (page 87), Stuffed Acorn Squash with Beef and Lentils (page 177), Sweet Potato Sheet Pan Nachos (page 145), Tomato and Red Bell Pepper Bruschetta (page 63), Tortellini with Mushroom Bolognese (page 151), Turkey-Stuffed Zucchini Boats (page 169), Watermelon, Tomato, and Cucumber Salad (page 86)

# Turnip

**Season:** Fall

**About the vegetable:** This white-and-purple root veggie has textures and flavors that are a mix between a potato and a radish, though they are actually members of the mustard family.

**How to select:** Look for turnips that feel heavy for their size and boast a bright, even color.

**How to prep:** Clean using a vegetable brush under running water; peel the skin on tougher, more mature turnips; and chop before cooking.

**How to store:** Keep in a plastic bag in the crisper drawer of the refrigerator for up to two weeks.

**Varieties to try:** Baby (all white), mature (purple and white)

**Pairs well with:** Butter, cheese, garlic, ginger, olive oil, other root vegetables, thyme

**Can easily be swapped with:** Parsnips, potatoes, rutabaga

**Watch out for:** Turnips have a little bit of heat to them, so mix with other root veggies, or mellow them out with flavors like ginger or garlic.

**Recipes:** Cauliflower and Root Vegetable Mash Bowls with Ground Beef (page 178), Cheesy Scalloped Potatoes and Turnips (page 81), Lemony Lentil-Turnip Soup (page 103), Lemony Turnip-Corn Soup (page 103), Roasted Root Salad (page 98), Sweet Potato and Root Vegetable Mash (page 79), Turnips au Gratin (page 80)

# Winter Greens (Collards, Kale, Swiss Chard)

**Season:** Winter

**About the vegetables:** These leafy greens are well known to be nutrient powerhouses, and they are extremely versatile, too. Use in a salad, smoothie, side dish, soup, or even as a sandwich wrap.

**How to select:** Look for bright-colored, lively-looking leaves with no wilting or discoloration.

**How to prep:** Wash thoroughly to remove dirt and grit, cut off the thick stems or ribs, then shred or slice as desired.

**How to store:** Keep in the crisper drawer in the refrigerator for up to five days.

**Varieties to try:** Escarole, mustard greens, rainbow chard

**Pairs well with:** Beef, cheese, chicken, fish, garlic, lemon, potatoes

**Can easily be swapped with:** Other leafy greens, like spinach

**Watch out for:** Plain and unseasoned leafy greens are bitter and hard to eat. Be sure to add fat and flavor and, in the case of kale, massage the leaves before serving. To massage, start by separating the leaves from the ribs and placing them in a large bowl with a drizzle of olive oil and a pinch of salt. Gently rub each leaf until all are lightly coated with oil and softened.

**Recipes:** Apple, Cheddar, and Collard Wraps (page 110), Autumn Roasted Vegetable Wraps (page 111), Black Bean and Kale Tortilla Soup (page 105), Collard and Lentil Soup (page 105), Creamy Kale-Artichoke Dip (page 71), Fall Harvest Mediterranean Salad (page 95), Fall Harvest Pizza (page 126), Foil-Wrapped Braised Kale (page 73), Garlicky Swiss Chard and Onions (page 74), Kale Artichoke Mac and Cheese (page 150), Kale Chimichurri (page 183), Lemony Lentil Soup with Kale (page 103), Mushroom-Kale Soup with White Beans and Farro (page 105), One-Pan Tuscan White Bean Skillet (page 128), Roasted Vegetable Salad with Goat Cheese (page 98), Spinach-Kale Pesto (page 182), Strawberry-Kale Salad (page 88), Super Green Guacamole (page 184), Sweet Potato–Kale Frittata (page 127), Tuna Collard Wraps (page 159), Tuscan Vegetable Pasta (page 120), Warm Kale Caesar Salad (page 93)

# Winter Squash (Acorn, Butternut, Spaghetti)

**Season:** Fall, winter

**About the vegetables:** Though they're named "winter" squash, most varieties come into season during the fall months and have a long shelf life. They'll last long enough for you to experiment with adding their deliciousness to baked goods, soups, and entrées.

**How to select:** Seek out squash with firm, intact skin and an attached stem to ensure that it's fresh (and hasn't been visited by bugs!).

**How to prep:** Cut off the stem, slice in half, and scoop out seeds.

**How to store:** Wipe down with a water and vinegar mixture to clean the skin and prevent mold/fungus from growing while you keep them in a cool, low-humidity area for several months.

**Varieties to try:** Blue Hubbard, delicata, kabocha, red kuri

**Pairs well with:** Bacon, carrots, cinnamon, brown sugar, ginger, honey, maple syrup, onions, rosemary, sage

**Can easily be swapped with:** Pumpkin

**Watch out for:** Winter squash can be intimidating and tough to cut. Start by slicing off the stem or end to create a flat surface, and place a damp towel under your cutting board to prevent sliding.

**Recipes:** Autumn Roasted Vegetable Wraps (page 111), Beef and Lentil Rice Bowl with Roasted Acorn Squash (page 177), Butternut Squash and Brown Rice Curry with Tofu (page 137), Butternut Squash and Apple Crisp (page 198), Butternut Squash Mac and Cheese (page 150), Fall Harvest Mediterranean Salad (page 95), Fall Harvest Pizza (page 126), Greek Stuffed Spaghetti Squash (page 122), Roasted Vegetable Ketchup (page 190), Roasted Vegetable Salad with Goat Cheese (page 83), Spaghetti Squash Burrito Bowls (page 121), Spaghetti Squash with Romesco (page 70), Spinach and White Bean Stuffed Spaghetti Squash (page 122), Squash and Sweet Potato Mash (page 79), Squash Frittata Bites (page 127), Stuffed Acorn Squash with Beef and Lentils (page 177), Stuffed Butternut Squash (page 177), Turkey-Stuffed Acorn Squash (page 170)

# Zucchini (and Summer Squash)

**Season:** Summer

**About the vegetables:** While some zucchini can grow really big, most are harvested early because their skin is softer, the seeds are edible, and the taste is less bitter. Zucchini and summer squash also grow an edible flower, called a squash blossom, which is delicious and often served stuffed and fried.

**How to select:** Look for small to medium-size shiny green (or yellow) zucchini without bruises or cuts. A little bit of prickly fuzz on the outside is fine.

**How to prep:** Wash, dry, and slice the ends off.

**How to store:** Keep in the refrigerator in a plastic bag for about a week.

**Varieties to try:** Green, golden

**Pairs well with:** Basil, cheese, eggplant, garlic, lemon, mushrooms, onions, tomatoes

**Can easily be swapped with:** Cucumber, eggplant

**Watch out for:** Like eggplant, zucchini has a high water content, so salt it and let it sit out for about 10 minutes before patting dry. This will help the zucchini soak up any flavors in your dish without weighing it down.

**Recipes:** Lasagna-Style Stuffed Zucchini (page 130), Parmesan Zucchini Chips (page 76), Pumpkin-Zucchini Crisp (page 198), Roasted Vegetable Ratatouille Soup (page 104), Sheet Pan Summer Squash and Shrimp (page 168), Shrimp en Papillote with Lemon Zucchini (page 155), Simple Ratatouille Soup (page 104), Southwest Zucchini Boats (page 170), Summer Grilled Vegetable Salad (page 98), Summer Slaw with Zucchini and Carrots (page 67), Summer Squash Soup (page 102), Turkey-Stuffed Zucchini Boats (page 169), Zucchini Bread Cookies (page 201), Zucchini Brownies (page 193), Zucchini-Radish Salsa (page 186), Zucchini Strips (page 72)

# PART THREE

# The Recipes

Crispy Eggplant Bites with Simple Marina Sauce, 72

# CHAPTER 4

# Snacks, Sides, and Small Bites

# Berry-Beet Smoothie

The beet-utiful, bright pink color of this smoothie should be enough to tempt anyone to give it a try. Add in the benefits of antioxidants, vitamin C, folate, and fiber, and this is a sweet sip that'll help you welcome the day.

SEASON:
Spring, summer, fall, winter

VEGAN

**Makes 2 smoothies | Prep time: 5 minutes | Cook time: 40 to 60 minutes**

2 beets, leaves and
    stems removed
¾ cup frozen mixed berries
1 banana
1 tablespoon chia or flaxseeds
¾ cup unsweetened
    almond milk

**PER SERVING:** Calories: 201; Total fat: 4g; Carbohydrates: 37g; Fiber: 8g; Protein: 6g; Calcium: 88mg; Vitamin D: 0mcg; Vitamin B$_{12}$: 0mcg; Iron: 2mg; Zinc: 1mg

1. Preheat the oven to 400°F.

2. Put the beets on a large piece of aluminum foil, folding it over to seal.

3. Roast in the oven for 40 to 60 minutes, or until tender. Cooking time will vary based on the size.

4. Allow the beets to cool, then use a paper towel or your hands to remove the skins.

5. Chop the beets into cubes. Put the beets, berries, banana, chia, and almond milk in a blender or food processor, and blend until smooth.

6. Enjoy immediately as a smoothie, or build your own smoothie bowl with optional toppings like sliced bananas, nuts, coconut shreds, and more.

➤ **Make it easier:** Save prep time for other dishes by roasting beets in advance, then chop and freeze them in freezer-safe bags. Store-bought, frozen beets are another convenient option.

**VARIATIONS:**

➤ **Pink Piña Colada Smoothie:** Swap the almond milk for coconut milk and the berries for frozen pineapple.
➤ **Pumpkin Power Smoothie:** Replace beets with beet greens or spinach, and swap the berries for pumpkin puree.

# Tomato and Red Bell Pepper Bruschetta

SEASON:
Summer

VEGAN

Fresh tomato and basil is one of my very favorite combinations, especially in the summer. If you can pick these ingredients right from a home garden, bam! You'll have a snazzy summer snack in no time. But don't let a lack of garden-fresh goodies stop you from running out to the store to make this easy and inexpensive bruschetta.

**Serves 6 to 8 | Prep time: 15 minutes | Cook time: 10 minutes**

3 tablespoons olive oil, plus more for brushing on the baguette

4 garlic cloves, minced

1 French baguette, sliced into ¼-to-½-inch slices

6 Roma tomatoes, finely diced

1 cup diced roasted red peppers

½ white onion, small dice

¼ cup fresh basil, chiffonade (cut into ribbon-like pieces)

½ teaspoon salt

¼ teaspoon freshly ground black pepper

1. Preheat the oven to 350°F.

2. In a small sauté pan or skillet, heat the olive oil over medium heat. Sauté the garlic for about 1 minute or until fragrant. Set aside.

3. Grease or line a sheet pan with parchment paper. Place slices of the baguette evenly on the sheet pan. Using a pastry brush, lightly brush each baguette slice with olive oil. Bake for 5 to 10 minutes, until golden brown.

4. In a large bowl, toss together the tomatoes, red peppers, onions, and reserved olive oil with garlic, basil, salt, and black pepper.

5. Spoon the toppings on toasted baguette slices just before serving.

CONTINUED

**PER SERVING:** Calories: 208; Total fat: 8g; Carbohydrates: 30g; Fiber: 3g; Protein: 6g; Calcium: 36mg; Vitamin D: 0mcg; Vitamin B$_{12}$: 0mcg; Iron: 2mg; Zinc: 1mg

## Tomato and Red Bell Pepper Bruschetta CONTINUED

➤ **Beyond the basics:** Roast your own red bell peppers by removing the seeds and stem, cutting in half, and placing them cut-side down on a sheet pan in a 400°F oven for 20 to 25 minutes. Allow to cool before removing skin and chopping as desired.

### VARIATIONS:

➤ **Grilled Chicken Bruschetta:** Skip the bread and serve fresh bruschetta topping over grilled chicken.

➤ **Greek Bruschetta:** To give this a Mediterranean flair, add in diced cucumbers, olives, and feta cheese, and leave out the basil.

# BLT Bites

These bite-size BLTs are quick and easy to toss together for your next picnic, barbecue, or family gathering. This recipe highlights the coveted summer tomato, holds the mayo, and lets the avocado create a creamy, satisfying surprise inside.

**SEASON:**
Summer

**VEGAN OPTION**
(See variation)

**Serves 4 to 6 | Prep time: 10 minutes | Cook time: 10 minutes**

6 slices bacon

12 Campari tomatoes

1 head romaine lettuce, washed and chopped

1 avocado, chopped

½ teaspoon salt

¼ teaspoon freshly ground black pepper

**PER SERVING:** Calories: 265; Total fat: 15g; Carbohydrates: 25g; Fiber: 12g; Protein: 13g; Calcium: 98mg; Vitamin D: 3mcg; Vitamin B$_{12}$: 0mcg; Iron: 3mg; Zinc: 2mg

1. Heat a sauté pan or skillet on medium heat and cook the bacon until crisp.

2. While the bacon is cooking, slice the stems off the tomatoes and use a spoon or small paring knife to scoop out the seeds and guts. Discard or reserve to use later in stocks and sauces. Place the tomatoes cut-side up on a plate or platter.

3. When the bacon is done cooking, put the slices on a paper towel to remove any excess grease. Chop finely.

4. In a small bowl, combine the chopped lettuce, bacon, and avocado. Season to taste with salt and pepper.

5. Fill the tomatoes with the bacon, lettuce, and avocado mixture, and serve.

➤ **Prep tip:** If your tomatoes are really round or wobbly, trim a little off the bottom to create a flat surface to fill and serve.

**VARIATIONS:**

➤ **Vegan BLT Bites:** Simply swap in chopped cooked tempeh bacon to make these vegan.

➤ **Mini Brussels and Bacon Bites:** Replace the tomatoes with roasted Brussels sprouts that have been sliced in half, placing the bacon in between each half like a mini sandwich.

# Broccoli-Pear Slaw

SEASON:
Winter

**VEGETARIAN,
VEGAN OPTION**
(see headnote)

With a passion for reducing food waste, I was determined to come up with a recipe beyond soup that utilizes or, in this case, *features* the tender, juicy broccoli stalk. Try this crunchy, slightly sweet, totally refreshing twist on coleslaw at your next barbecue or potluck. To make this vegan, opt for vegan mayo.

**Serves 4 | Prep time: 10 minutes**

1 medium head broccoli

1 pear, any type, cored

1 teaspoon lemon juice

½ cup mayonnaise

2 tablespoons apple
   cider vinegar

Salt

Freshly ground black pepper

¼ cup dried cranberries

---

**PER SERVING:** Calories: 276;
Total fat: 21g; Carbohydrates: 21g;
Fiber: 5g; Protein: 4g; Calcium: 61mg;
Vitamin D: 2mcg; Vitamin B$_{12}$: 0mcg;
Iron: 1mg; Zinc: 1mg

1. Prep the broccoli by chopping the florets, then peeling or slicing away the outer hearty leaves and tough bottom of the stem. Julienne the stem and the pear, and toss them in a medium bowl with lemon juice.

2. In a separate small bowl, mix together the mayonnaise, vinegar, salt, and pepper.

3. Pour the dressing over the broccoli-pear mixture, stirring to coat evenly. Mix in the dried cranberries and serve.

➤ **Prep tip:** Save the broccoli stems for this dish when making another broccoli recipe that calls for only florets, such as Root-to-Stem Rainbow Salad with Easy Herb Vinaigrette (page 96) or Broccoli-Cheddar Stuffed Potatoes (page 123).

**VARIATIONS:**

➤ **Sweet Sprout Slaw:** Swap the broccoli for shaved Brussels sprouts and add a drizzle of honey.

➤ **Summer Slaw with Zucchini and Carrots:** Replace the broccoli with julienned zucchini and carrot sticks for a summery twist on this winter slaw.

# Rutabaga Fries

SEASON:
Fall, winter

**VEGAN**

It's root, root, root for these rutabaga fries! If you don't try them, that's a shame. Rutabaga is surprisingly rich in vitamin C, plus it offers potassium, B vitamins, and iron. These fries are flavorful enough to enjoy all on their own, or try them with the Spicy Beet Ketchup on page 190.

**Serves 4 | Prep time: 10 minutes | Cook time: 30 minutes**

1 large rutabaga, peeled and
   cut into spears
2 tablespoons olive oil
2 teaspoons paprika
1 teaspoon garlic powder
½ teaspoon salt
¼ teaspoon freshly ground
   black pepper

**PER SERVING:** Calories: 137; Total fat: 7g; Carbohydrates: 18g; Fiber: 5g; Protein: 2g; Calcium: 86mg; Vitamin D: 0mcg; Vitamin B$_{12}$: 0mcg; Iron: 1mg; Zinc: 0mg

1. Preheat the oven to 425°F. Grease or line a sheet pan with parchment paper.

2. In a large bowl, toss together the rutabaga spears, olive oil, paprika, garlic powder, salt, and pepper.

3. Evenly lay the rutabaga on the sheet pan. (Don't over-crowd the pan. Use an additional sheet pan, if needed.)

4. Bake for 30 minutes, flipping halfway through the cook time.

➤ **Prep tip:** A ripe rutabaga will usually have purple-tinged skin. If you scratch the skin slightly, you should see yellow flesh beneath. Stay away from rutabagas that are bruised or blemished.

**VARIATIONS:**

➤ **Carrot Fries:** Trade out rutabaga for sliced carrots.
➤ **Italian Rutabaga Fries:** Try different seasonings like dried basil, oregano, and parsley for an Italian twist.

# Cauliflower Steaks with Romesco Sauce

SEASON:
Fall, winter, spring

VEGAN

Cauliflower has gained popularity as a low-carb substitute for rice and potatoes, but this recipe allows us to celebrate the cauliflower just as it is. Slicing the cauliflower into "steaks," rather than chopping it into florets, creates a delicious display for anything from beans to poultry to fish. In this case, the cauliflower steaks are drizzled with romesco, which adds color and flavor.

**Serves 6 | Prep time: 10 minutes | Cook time: 25 minutes**

2 heads cauliflower

¼ cup olive oil

1 teaspoon garlic powder

1 teaspoon onion powder

¼ teaspoon salt

¼ teaspoon freshly ground
   black pepper

1 batch Romesco Sauce
   (page 187)

½ cup chopped fresh basil

**PER SERVING:** Calories: 211;
Total fat: 17g; Carbohydrates: 13g;
Fiber: 6g; Protein: 5g; Calcium: 86mg;
Vitamin D: 0mcg; Vitamin B₁₂: 0mcg;
Iron: 2mg; Zinc: 1mg

1. Preheat the oven to 450°F. Grease or line 2 large sheet pans with parchment paper.

2. Remove the leaves and stem end of the cauliflower, still leaving the cauliflower fully intact.

3. Place the stem-end down on the cutting board and slice the cauliflower into "steaks," 1 to 2 inches in width.

4. Arrange the steaks on the sheet pans, making sure they are not overlapping.

5. In a small bowl, whisk together the olive oil, garlic powder, onion powder, salt, and pepper.

6. Using a pastry brush, coat both sides of the steak with the oil mixture.

7. Place the sheet pans in the oven and roast for 10 minutes. Flip the cauliflower and bake for 10 to 15 minutes more, until fork-tender and golden brown.

8. Transfer the steaks to a platter, top with romesco sauce, and sprinkle with basil.

CONTINUED

# Cauliflower Steaks with Romesco Sauce CONTINUED

➤ **Prep tip:** Be sure to cut cauliflower steaks approximately the same width for even cooking.

## VARIATIONS:

➤ **Spaghetti Squash with Romesco:** The romesco sauce goes well on spaghetti squash, too. Cut the squash in half lengthwise, scoop out the seeds, drizzle it with olive oil, season with salt and pepper, and pop it into a preheated oven for about 45 minutes at 400°F. Top with romesco and enjoy!

➤ **Roasted Asparagus with Romesco:** Coat asparagus spears with oil, garlic powder, and onion powder, and season with salt and pepper. Roast for 10 to 15 minutes at 400°F and top with romesco.

# Creamy Kale-Artichoke Dip

SEASON:
Winter, spring

**VEGETARIAN**

Dips and sauces are often used as a way to get kids and adults alike to eat more vegetables. You certainly can use crunchy veggies like radish, celery, and bell pepper as a vessel to enjoy this creamy dip, but because it's already packed with all the goodness of kale, artichokes, and carrots, you can also serve it with crispy tortilla or pita chips—or enjoy by the spoonful.

**Makes 3½ cups | Prep time: 10 minutes | Cook time: 20 minutes**

1½ cups chopped kale

1 (6-ounce) jar marinated artichoke hearts, drained and chopped

1 medium carrot, shredded

2 garlic cloves, minced

2 cups plain Greek yogurt

½ cup mayonnaise

1 teaspoon salt

½ teaspoon freshly ground black pepper

¼ teaspoon onion powder

¼ teaspoon smoked paprika

**PER SERVING (½ CUP):**
Calories: 170; Total fat: 14g; Carbohydrates: 8g; Fiber: 3g; Protein: 4g; Calcium: 101mg; Vitamin D: 3mcg; Vitamin B$_{12}$: 0mcg; Iron: 0mg; Zinc: 1mg

1. Combine the kale, artichoke hearts, carrot, garlic, Greek yogurt, mayonnaise, salt, pepper, onion powder, and paprika in a bowl and mix well.

2. Serve immediately or, if preferred warm, transfer to an oven-safe dish and bake for 20 minutes at 350°F.

➤ **Beyond the basics:** For a creamier consistency, combine all ingredients in a food processor or blender and pulse until smooth. If baking, sprinkle Parmesan cheese for a salty and crispy top.

**VARIATIONS:**

➤ **Creamy Beet Dip:** Ditch the kale and sub in 8 ounces of roasted beets, along with a drizzle of honey or whipped feta cheese.

➤ **Baba Ghanoush:** Swap kale, artichoke, and carrots for 2 roasted eggplants, use only 1 cup of Greek yogurt, and add 2 tablespoons of lemon juice.

# Crispy Eggplant Bites

SEASON:
Fall

**VEGETARIAN**

These crispy, crunchy bites are an easy way to both serve and eat more plants, and they'll quickly become your new favorite way to enjoy eggplant. Leave the skin on for extra fiber and an antioxidant boost from anthocyanin, which is the reason why the eggplant has its beautiful purple hue.

**Serves 4 to 6 | Prep time: 40 minutes | Cook time: 30 minutes**

2 tablespoons salt, divided

1 large eggplant, cubed

¾ cup whole-wheat flour

3 large eggs

½ teaspoon freshly ground black pepper

1 teaspoon dried oregano

1 teaspoon dried rosemary

½ teaspoon dried thyme

1 teaspoon garlic powder

2½ cups panko bread crumbs

Simple Marinara Sauce (page 72), for serving (optional)

**PER SERVING:** Calories: 356; Total fat: 7g; Carbohydrates: 59g; Fiber: 9g; Protein: 15g; Calcium: 140mg; Vitamin D: 31mcg; Vitamin B$_{12}$: 1mcg; Iron: 4mg; Zinc: 2mg

1. Preheat the oven to 400°F. Sprinkle 1 tablespoon of salt over the cubed eggplant and let sit for 30 minutes, then pat dry with a paper towel.

2. Pour the flour into one mixing bowl and, in a separate small bowl, beat the eggs. In a third bowl, combine the pepper, oregano, rosemary, thyme, garlic powder, and bread crumbs.

3. Dredge the eggplant cubes in the flour, then the egg wash, and finally the bread crumb mixture.

4. Spread evenly on a sheet pan and cook for 30 minutes, using a spatula to turn halfway through.

5. Enjoy with marinara sauce, if using.

➤ **Prep tip:** Dredging can quickly become a messy activity, so keep a small bowl of water nearby to rinse off your fingers between batches.

**VARIATIONS:**

➤ **Zucchini Strips:** Replace eggplant with sliced zucchini strips, remembering to salt the zucchini prior to dredging in flour, egg, and the bread crumb mixture.

➤ **Crispy Mushrooms:** Sub in button mushrooms for the eggplant for a perfectly poppable appetizer.

# Foil-Wrapped Braised Cabbage

SEASON:
Fall, winter, spring

VEGAN

With just four ingredients and set-it-and-forget-it instructions, these little foil-wrapped gifts are a great way to expand your cabbage repertoire beyond summer slaw and St. Patrick's Day fare. Cabbage is an excellent source of vitamin C, fiber, and potassium. But wait, there's more! It's also chock-full of anthocyanins (found in red cabbage) and amino acids like glutamine that help lower the risk of cancers and decrease inflammation.

**Serves 4 | Prep time: 10 minutes | Cook time: 45 minutes**

1 head cabbage, quartered, core intact

4 tablespoons sesame oil, divided

4 tablespoons low-sodium soy sauce, divided

2 tablespoons low-sodium vegetable broth, divided

1. Preheat the oven to 400°F.
2. Place each cabbage wedge on a piece of aluminum foil.
3. Drizzle the sides of each wedge with 1 tablespoon of sesame oil and soy sauce and ½ tablespoon of vegetable broth.
4. Wrap each foil packet tightly. Place on a sheet pan.
5. Roast the packets in the oven for 45 minutes.

**PER SERVING:** Calories: 185; Total fat: 14g; Carbohydrates: 14g; Fiber: 6g; Protein: 4g; Calcium: 95mg; Vitamin D: 0mcg; Vitamin $B_{12}$: 0mcg; Iron: 1mg; Zinc: 1mg

➤ **Prep tip:** Keep the core intact to keep all the leaves from separating.

## VARIATIONS:

➤ **Braised Root Vegetables:** Swap cabbage for root veggies like carrots, radishes, and turnips.

➤ **Foil-Wrapped Braised Kale:** Replace the cabbage with a head of kale, stems removed.

# Garlicky Swiss Chard and Onions

SEASON:
Summer, fall

**VEGAN**

This dish is so simple it should barely count as a recipe. I'm putting it in here anyway because I don't want you to miss out on the simple goodness of leafy green vegetables with garlic, olive oil, and salt. The onion adds a touch of sweetness and, if you want some heat, you can add red pepper flakes or cayenne before serving.

**Serves 4 to 6 | Prep time: 5 minutes | Cook time: 5 minutes**

2 tablespoons olive oil

3 garlic cloves, minced

1 sweet yellow onion, sliced

2 bunches Swiss chard, leaves and stems separated, both roughly chopped

1 teaspoon salt

**PER SERVING:** Calories: 103; Total fat: 7g; Carbohydrates: 10g; Fiber: 2g; Protein: 2g; Calcium: 57mg; Vitamin D: 0mcg; Vitamin $B_{12}$: 0mcg; Iron: 2mg; Zinc: 0mg

1. In a sauté pan or skillet over medium-high heat, heat the olive oil.

2. Add in the garlic, sliced onion, and chard stems, and sauté for 2 minutes.

3. Add in the chard leaves and salt, then stir and cook for another 2 to 3 minutes, or until the chard is wilted.

➤ **Make it easier:** Grab a bag of frozen Swiss chard or another hardy green vegetable like collards or kale for this recipe.

**VARIATIONS:**

➤ **Lovely Leeks with Garlic:** Substitute chopped leeks for the Swiss chard for more of a spring twist on this side.

➤ **Garlicky Green Beans:** Replace the Swiss chard with fresh green beans for an extra dose of crunchiness.

# Honey-Sriracha Brussels Sprouts

SEASON:
Fall

VEGETARIAN

If you *think* you don't like Brussels sprouts, this recipe is here to change your mind. The sweet and spicy combo of honey and sriracha doesn't hide but instead highlights the savory, nutty taste of the Brussels sprouts. Try serving these at your next gathering to convert all the sprout haters in your life.

**Serves 4 | Prep time: 5 minutes | Cook time: 30 minutes**

1 pound Brussels sprouts, trimmed and halved

2 tablespoons olive oil

½ teaspoon salt

¼ teaspoon freshly ground black pepper

1 tablespoon honey

2 tablespoons sriracha

**PER SERVING:** Calories: 125; Total fat: 7g; Carbohydrates: 15g; Fiber: 4g; Protein: 4g; Calcium: 49mg; Vitamin D: 0mcg; Vitamin $B_{12}$: 0mcg; Iron: 2mg; Zinc: 1mg

1. Preheat the oven to 375°F. Spread the Brussels sprouts evenly on a sheet pan, drizzle with olive oil, then season with salt and pepper.

2. Bake for 25 to 30 minutes, or until the leaves begin to brown and the sprouts are fork-tender.

3. While the sprouts are baking, whisk the honey and sriracha in a large bowl. Add in the cooked Brussels sprouts and toss to coat.

4. Return the sprouts to the pan and bake 5 minutes more.

➤ **Beyond the basics:** For extra crispy sprouts, heat the sheet pan in the oven as you preheat so it's ready to go.

**VARIATIONS:**

➤ **Sweet and Spicy Cauliflower:** Keep the recipe as is, but swap in chopped cauliflower for Brussels sprouts.

➤ **Balsamic Maple Brussels Sprouts:** Roast the Brussels sprouts following the recipe and replace the honey and sriracha with balsamic vinegar and maple syrup.

# Parmesan Zucchini Chips

SEASON:
Summer

**VEGETARIAN**

These cheesy, crunchy veggie chips are an easy way to use up any extra summer squash you might have lying around. The Italian herbs and cheese pair well with the Simple Marinara Sauce on page 185.

**Serves 4 to 6 | Prep time: 20 minutes | Cook time: 25 minutes**

3 large zucchini

2 eggs

½ cup panko bread crumbs

⅓ cup grated Parmesan cheese

1 tablespoon Italian seasoning

½ teaspoon salt

¼ teaspoon freshly ground
    black pepper

Simple Marinara Sauce
    (page 185), for dipping

**PER SERVING:** Calories: 170;
Total fat: 6g; Carbohydrates: 20g;
Fiber: 5g; Protein: 11g; Calcium: 153mg;
Vitamin D: 22mcg; Vitamin B$_{12}$: 0mcg;
Iron: 3mg; Zinc: 2mg

1. Preheat the oven to 400°F. Grease or line 2 sheet pans with parchment paper.

2. Slice the zucchini into rounds about ¼ inch thick. Lay the rounds on a flat surface and leave for 5 to 10 minutes, so the moisture releases. Pat dry with a paper towel.

3. In a small bowl, whisk the eggs. In another bowl, mix together the panko, Parmesan, Italian seasoning, salt, and pepper.

4. Dip the zucchini rounds into the eggs to coat both sides, letting the excess egg drip off. Add to the panko mixture and coat the zucchini rounds on both sides, gently pressing the mixture into the zucchini. Place the rounds in rows on the prepared sheet pans. Repeat until all the zucchini is coated.

5. Bake for 20 to 25 minutes, or until golden and crisp. Serve alongside Simple Marinara Sauce, if desired.

➢ **Prep tip:** Peel the zucchini before slicing it to create more surface area for the breading to stick to.

---

## VARIATIONS:

➢ **Baked Parmesan Asparagus Fries:** Swap zucchini slices with asparagus spears, and bake for 10 to 12 minutes.

➢ **Salt and Vinegar Cucumber Chips:** Salt a sliced cucumber, let it sit for 10 minutes, and then pat it dry. Dip the cucumber slices into apple cider vinegar, sprinkle them with more salt, and spread them on a sheet pan. Bake at 200°F for 3 hours, or until the chips are dry and crispy.

# Snow Pea and Carrot Sauté

SEASON:
Spring, summer,
fall, winter

VEGAN

This quick and easy side dish pairs well with almost any entrée you can dream up, and is readily available year-round. Try this over rice and beef for a touch of salty sweetness and crunch.

**Serves 4 | Prep time: 5 minutes | Cook time: 5 minutes**

2 teaspoons sesame oil

2 cups snow peas,
 strings removed

1 cup julienned carrots

2 scallions, chopped

1 teaspoon grated fresh ginger

1 tablespoon low-sodium
 soy sauce

Salt

Freshly ground black pepper

Sesame seeds (optional)

**PER SERVING:** Calories: 37;
Total fat: 2g; Carbohydrates: 4g;
Fiber: 1g; Protein: 1g; Calcium: 16mg;
Vitamin D: 0mcg; Vitamin B$_{12}$: 0mcg;
Iron: 0mg; Zinc: 0mg

1. In a large sauté pan or skillet, heat the sesame oil over medium-high. Add the snow peas and carrots and cook 4 to 5 minutes, or until tender.

2. Stir in the scallions, ginger, and soy sauce and cook for 1 more minute.

3. Season with salt and pepper to taste. Sprinkle with sesame seeds, if using.

➤ **Prep tip:** The stringy part of the snow peas tends to be chewy, so remove it by taking each snow pea and pulling the small tip at one end. Pull it against the flatter side, not the rounder side, of the snow pea. It'll remove the string along that side.

## VARIATIONS:

➤ **Green Bean and Carrot Sauté:** Switch up the flavor by using green beans instead of snow peas.
➤ **Carrot and Bok Choy Sauté:** Use bok choy in place of snow peas, adding them in after the carrots have cooked for 2 to 3 minutes.

# Sweet Potato–Pumpkin Mash

SEASON:
Fall, winter

**VEGETARIAN**

Think beyond the piecrust when it comes to these two versatile fall favorites. This delicious mash-up is a healthy way to get your fill of fiber, vitamin A, vitamin C, as well as key nutrients like potassium and magnesium.

**Serves 6 | Prep time: 20 minutes | Cook time: 15 minutes**

1½ pounds sweet potatoes, peeled and cubed

1 sprig rosemary

2 tablespoons salted butter

1 cup canned pumpkin puree

1 tablespoon maple syrup

½ teaspoon salt

1 garlic clove, grated

¼ teaspoon ground cinnamon

**PER SERVING:** Calories: 155; Total fat: 4g; Carbohydrates: 29g; Fiber: 5g; Protein: 2g; Calcium: 41mg; Vitamin D: 3mcg; Vitamin B$_{12}$: 0mcg; Iron: 1mg; Zinc: 0mg

1. In a large pot, put the sweet potatoes and rosemary with enough cold water to cover them. Cover the pot and bring to a boil. Reduce the heat to low and cook for 15 minutes, or until the potatoes are fork-tender.

2. Drain the potatoes, put them in a separate bowl, and set aside.

3. While the pot is still hot, add in the butter and let it melt. Stir in the pumpkin puree, maple syrup, salt, garlic, and cinnamon. Stir to combine.

4. Add the potatoes back to the pot and use a potato masher to reach desired consistency. For a creamier texture, use an immersion blender.

➤ **Prep tip:** Make sure to use pure pumpkin puree, not pumpkin pie filling. Be careful—they sit next to each other on the grocery shelf.

**VARIATIONS:**

➤ **Squash and Sweet Potato Mash:** Replace the pumpkin puree with mashed butternut squash.
➤ **Sweet Potato and Root Vegetable Mash:** Add mashed roasted root vegetables like carrots, turnips, and parsnips in with sweet potatoes.

# Turnips au Gratin

I promise you no one will be upset when you "turnip" to a family gathering with this dish. Cheesy puns aside, these comforting, satisfying, and, yes, cheesy scalloped root veggies are also full of protein, fiber, and flavor.

SEASON:
Fall, winter

**VEGETARIAN**

**Serves 6 | Prep time: 20 minutes | Cook time: 75 minutes**

3 tablespoons unsalted butter

1 large onion, thinly sliced

4 garlic cloves, minced

¼ cup all-purpose flour

1 cup low-sodium
  vegetable broth

2 cups whole milk

1 teaspoon salt

½ teaspoon freshly ground
  black pepper

3 pounds turnips, peeled and
  sliced into ⅛-inch rounds

2 cups shredded sharp
  cheddar cheese

Chopped fresh
  parsley (optional)

**PER SERVING:** Calories: 349;
Total fat: 21g; Carbohydrates: 26g;
Fiber: 5g; Protein: 14g;
Calcium: 426mg; Vitamin D: 15mcg;
Vitamin B$_{12}$: 1mcg; Iron: 1mg;
Zinc: 2mg

1. Preheat the oven to 400°F. Coat a 9-by-13-inch baking dish with cooking spray. Set aside.

2. Heat a large sauté pan or skillet over medium-high heat. Melt the butter until bubbly and foamy. Add the onion and sauté for about 5 minutes, until soft and translucent. Add the garlic and sauté 1 minute more, until fragrant.

3. Sprinkle the flour over the onions and garlic, and stir until coated. Cook for about 1 minute. Slowly pour in the broth and whisk until combined. Then slowly whisk in the milk. Stir in the salt and pepper. Continue to cook and whisk for about 2 minutes as the mixture just begins to gently simmer and thicken. (Do not let the mixture come to a boil.) Remove from the heat and set aside.

4. Create an even layer of turnips at the bottom of the baking dish. (It's okay if a few of the edges overlap.) Add a thin layer of the cream sauce. Sprinkle evenly with some of the cheese. Repeat the layering process until all turnips are used and finish with cheddar cheese on top.

5.  Cover the baking dish with foil and bake for 45 minutes. Remove foil and bake uncovered for 20 to 30 minutes more, until the turnips are cooked through and the cheese on top has browned.

6.  Remove from the oven and sprinkle with parsley, if using.

➤ **Beyond the basics:** Mix 1 cup of panko bread crumbs with parsley and toast in a pan for 5 to 10 minutes. Sprinkle on the baked turnips for a crunchy topping.

---

## VARIATIONS:

➤ **Cheesy Scalloped Potatoes and Turnips:** Use half potatoes and half turnips for an ode to the traditional dish.

➤ **Parsnips au Gratin:** Swap the turnips for parsnips and cheddar cheese for Gruyère in another unique twist.

Root-to-Stem Rainbow Salad with Easy Herb Vinaigrette, 96

# CHAPTER 5

# Salads and Soups

# Sweet Cucumber Salad with Toasted Sesame Oil

SEASON:
Summer

**VEGETARIAN**

It doesn't get any easier than this six-ingredient, crunchy cucumber salad. It's fast, sweet, and spicy, and you'll want to make it again and again during the summer when cucumbers are abundant. Pair it with Sweet Potato Burgers (page 143) or Salmon Cakes (page 160).

**Serves 4 | Prep time: 10 minutes**

4 cups seedless cucumbers, thinly sliced

¼ cup rice wine vinegar

1 teaspoon honey

½ teaspoon toasted sesame oil

¼ teaspoon salt

¼ teaspoon red pepper flakes

**PER SERVING:** Calories: 28; Total fat: 1g; Carbohydrates: 4g; Fiber: 1g; Protein: 1g; Calcium: 18mg; Vitamin D: 0mcg; Vitamin B$_{12}$: 0mcg; Iron: 0mg; Zinc: 0mg

1. Put the cucumbers in a large bowl.

2. In a small bowl, whisk together the rice vinegar, honey, sesame oil, salt, and red pepper flakes.

3. Add the dressing to the cucumbers and toss together. Cover and let sit in the refrigerator for at least 1 hour for the flavors to marinate.

➤ **Prep tip:** Use a mandoline to quickly and thinly slice the cucumbers.

**VARIATIONS:**

➤ **Creamy Cucumber-Onion Salad:** Mix sliced cucumbers with 1 sliced red onion, ½ cup of Greek yogurt, 1 teaspoon of honey, 2 tablespoons of chopped dill, and salt and pepper to taste.

➤ **Simple Kachumber Salad:** To make kachumber, which originated in India, combine cucumbers, ½ cup of tomatoes, ½ cup of chopped onions, and ¼ cup of shredded carrots with a squeeze of lemon juice and a sprinkle of cumin.

# Sweet and Spicy Citrus Salad

**SEASON:**
Spring, summer, fall, winter

**VEGETARIAN**

A little bit spicy, a little bit sweet, this is a refreshing side salad for a hot summer day. It's chock-full of nutrients like fiber, vitamins C and K, and potassium, and enjoying veggies like arugula and radishes combined with citrus fruit can have benefits for immunity, digestion, blood pressure, and more.

**Serves 4 to 6 | Prep time: 15 minutes**

### FOR THE SALAD

5 ounces arugula
   (about 6 cups)
4 or 5 small radishes, sliced
2 large oranges, skinned
   and sectioned

### FOR THE DRESSING

½ cup plain Greek yogurt
1 teaspoon Dijon mustard
2 tablespoons lemon juice
1 teaspoon honey
½ teaspoon salt
¼ teaspoon freshly ground
   black pepper

**PER SERVING:** Calories: 79; Total fat: 1g; Carbohydrates: 16g; Fiber: 3g; Protein: 3g; Calcium: 133mg; Vitamin D: 1mcg; Vitamin B$_{12}$: 0mcg; Iron: 1mg; Zinc: 0mg

1. **To make the salad:** Combine the arugula, radishes, and orange sections in a large bowl and toss.

2. **To make the dressing:** In a separate small bowl, whisk together the yogurt, mustard, lemon juice, honey, salt, and pepper.

3. Drizzle the dressing over the salad and toss to evenly coat. Divide and serve. Store leftovers in the refrigerator for 1 to 2 days.

➤ **Prep tip:** Radishes sliced in advance can become dry, so store them in a small bowl of cold water in the refrigerator.

### VARIATIONS:

➤ **Sweet and Spicy Berry Salad:** Replace the orange slices with cut strawberries and add some chopped mint into the arugula mix.

➤ **Stone Fruit Spicy Salad:** Use stone fruit like apricots or peaches in place of citrus and add half a jalapeño, seeded and diced.

# Watermelon-Jicama Salad

SEASON:
Summer

**VEGETARIAN**

You probably know it's important to stay hydrated, in addition to eating plenty of vegetables and fruits. Between the cucumber, jicama, and watermelon, this juicy salad does a wonderful job of helping you reach your hydration goals. It has a naturally high water content and is extremely flavorful. Serve this with grilled fish or chicken for a picture-perfect summer meal.

**Serves 4 | Prep time: 15 minutes**

4 cups cubed watermelon

2 mini cucumbers, sliced

1 cup peeled and julienned jicama

1 tablespoon olive oil

Juice from 1 lime

½ teaspoon ground cumin

¼ teaspoon salt

2 tablespoons chopped fresh mint

2 ounces feta cheese

1. In a large bowl, combine the watermelon, cucumbers, and jicama.

2. In a small bowl, whisk together the olive oil, lime juice, ground cumin, and salt. Pour over the watermelon mixture and toss gently to combine.

3. Add the mint and feta cheese just before serving. Toss gently to combine.

➤ **Prep tip:** Watermelon can be cut up to 5 days in advance and stored in glass or plastic containers in the refrigerator.

**PER SERVING:** Calories: 136; Total fat: 7g; Carbohydrates: 17g; Fiber: 3g; Protein: 4g; Calcium: 96mg; Vitamin D: 2mcg; Vitamin B$_{12}$: 0mcg; Iron: 1mg; Zinc: 1mg

**VARIATIONS:**

➤ **Watermelon-Jicama Skewers:** Dice the fruits and vegetables into cubes and put them on skewers for a fun appetizer.

➤ **Watermelon, Tomato, and Cucumber Salad:** No jicama? No problem! Just swap jicama with diced tomato.

# Spring Salad with Asparagus and Peas

SEASON:
Spring

**VEGAN**

All my favorite spring vegetables come together in this lovely, light salad. Over time, the veggies continue to soak up the flavors in the dressing, making it even more delectable. Shaved raw asparagus makes for a fancy salad, but if you prefer to chop instead of shave, boil the asparagus for 4 to 5 minutes before giving it an ice bath to prep for the salad.

**Serves 4 to 6 | Prep time: 10 minutes**

2 bunches asparagus, shaved

½ pound green beans, chopped (about 1½ cups)

6 ounces sugar snap peas

6 ounces cherry tomatoes, halved

2 tablespoons lemon juice

2 tablespoons Dijon mustard

1 tablespoon olive oil

**PER SERVING:** Calories: 98; Total fat: 4g; Carbohydrates: 14g; Fiber: 6g; Protein: 5g; Calcium: 72mg; Vitamin D: 0mcg; Vitamin B$_{12}$: 0mcg; Iron: 4mg; Zinc: 1mg

1. Combine the asparagus shavings, green beans, snap peas, and tomatoes in a large bowl.

2. In a separate bowl, whisk together the lemon juice, Dijon, and olive oil.

3. Drizzle the dressing over vegetables and toss to coat evenly.

➤ **Prep tip:** Hold the asparagus stem against a flat handle of a wooden spoon and use a vegetable peeler to shave from the base to the tip.

**VARIATIONS:**

➤ **Minty Green Spring Salad:** Add 2 cups of cooked whole-wheat farfalle pasta and 2 tablespoons of chopped mint leaves for a fresh and flavorful pasta salad.

➤ **Warmed Spring Salad with Parmesan:** Preheat the oven to 350°F and put all the vegetables on a sheet pan. Drizzle with lemon, Dijon, and olive oil. Bake for 5 to 7 minutes, and top with 1 to 2 ounces of shaved Parmesan before serving.

# Strawberry, Spinach, and Cucumber Salad

SEASON:
Summer

VEGETARIAN

Stay as cool as a cucumber with this summer salad, which has a powerful pairing of iron-rich spinach and strawberries packed with vitamin C. A simple vinaigrette finishes the flavor, but you could also try this salad with a creamy yogurt-based dressing, such as the one in the Sweet and Spicy Citrus Salad (page 85).

**Serves 4 | Prep time: 15 minutes**

## FOR THE SALAD

6 cups baby spinach

1 English cucumber, thinly sliced

1 cup sliced strawberries

3 ounces feta cheese

⅓ cup chopped walnuts

## FOR THE VINAIGRETTE

¼ cup olive oil

1 tablespoon apple cider vinegar

1 tablespoon honey

1 tablespoon Dijon mustard

Salt

Freshly ground black pepper

PER SERVING: Calories: 293; Total fat: 24g; Carbohydrates: 14g; Fiber: 3g; Protein: 7g; Calcium: 181mg; Vitamin D: 3mcg; Vitamin B₁₂: 0mcg; Iron: 2mg; Zinc: 1mg

1. **To make the salad:** In a large bowl, toss together the spinach, cucumber, and strawberries.

2. **To make the vinaigrette:** In a small bowl, whisk together the olive oil, apple cider vinegar, honey, and Dijon mustard. Season with salt and pepper to taste.

3. Drizzle dressing over salad. Top with feta and walnuts. Toss gently until incorporated.

➤ **Make it easier:** Prep a larger batch of the salad dressing in advance and keep in a sealed container in the refrigerator for up to 1 week.

### VARIATIONS:

➤ **Strawberry-Kale Salad:** For a crunchier, deeper green salad, opt for baby kale leaves instead of spinach.

➤ **Fall Spinach Salad:** Replace the strawberries with sliced pear and the cucumber with chopped celery. Swap goat cheese and pecans for the feta and walnuts, too.

# Black Bean and Corn Salad

SEASON:
Summer

**VEGAN**

Black beans offer up protein, and corn contributes key B vitamins and insoluble fiber for better digestion. Roma tomatoes are less water-packed than other varieties, preventing the flavors from becoming watered down. Served cold or hot, this bean and veggie salad works well for your next picnic, on top of meat or baked potatoes, or even as a salsa over nachos.

**Serves 6 | Prep time: 15 minutes**

2 (15-ounce) cans black beans, drained and rinsed

2 cups frozen corn, thawed

4 Roma tomatoes, diced

3 scallions, both white and green parts, chopped

2 avocados, diced

½ cup chopped cilantro

Juice from 2 limes

1 tablespoon avocado oil or olive oil

¼ teaspoon ground cumin

½ teaspoon chili powder

Salt

Freshly ground black pepper

**PER SERVING:** Calories: 332; Total fat: 14g; Carbohydrates: 46g; Fiber: 16g; Protein: 13g; Calcium: 54mg; Vitamin D: 0mcg; Vitamin $B_{12}$: 0mcg; Iron: 3mg; Zinc: 2mg

1.  In a large bowl, mix together the black beans, corn, tomatoes, and scallions. Gently fold in the avocados and cilantro.

2.  In a small bowl, whisk together the lime juice, oil, cumin, and chili powder. Drizzle the dressing over the bean salad and gently toss together.

3.  Season with salt and pepper to taste.

➤ **Prep tip:** Make this salad ahead of time and let the flavors soak in. Just leave the avocado and cilantro out, tossing them in before serving.

## VARIATIONS:

➤ **Black Bean and Cucumber Salad :** No corn? No problem. Chop up 1 cucumber for an equally sweet and refreshing salad.

➤ **Crunchy Black Bean and Corn Salad:** Sub tomatoes for colorful diced green and red bell peppers.

# Endive-Walnut Salad

SEASON:
Fall

VEGETARIAN

Endive, one of the more underutilized lettuces, shows up as the star in this salad with a combo of sweet and tangy flavors. Endive is high in vitamin K, an important nutrient for bone health, and has phytonutrients that help fight inflammation. This nutritious salad will quickly become a favorite.

**Serves 4 | Prep time: 15 minutes**

**FOR THE SALAD**

4 Belgian endive heads

2 ripe pears, sliced thin

¾ cup chopped walnuts

4 ounces blue
   cheese, crumbled

**FOR THE DRESSING**

2 tablespoons white
   wine vinegar

½ tablespoon Dijon mustard

¼ teaspoon salt

⅛ teaspoon freshly ground
   black pepper

3 tablespoons olive oil

**PER SERVING:** Calories: 404; Total fat: 33g; Carbohydrates: 21g; Fiber: 7g; Protein: 11g; Calcium: 233mg; Vitamin D: 6mcg; Vitamin B$_{12}$: 0mcg; Iron: 2mg; Zinc: 2mg

1. **To make the salad:** Cut off the root end of the endive, then slice it across the width into about ½-inch-thick slices. Put the slices in a large bowl of cold water to remove any excess dirt stuck in between the leaves, and separate the leaves in the process. Remove them from the water and spin in a salad spinner or pat dry.

2. **To make the dressing:** In a small mason jar, combine the vinegar, Dijon, salt, pepper, and olive oil. Secure the lid and shake well until combined.

3. In a large bowl, toss together the endive, pears, walnuts, and blue cheese. Drizzle with dressing and toss just before serving.

> **Beyond the basics:** Try leaving the endive leaves whole and fill them with pears, walnuts, and blue cheese. Drizzle the dressing over the top or serve on the side as a dip.

**VARIATIONS:**

> **Radicchio Pear Walnut Salad:** Replace the endive with radicchio for a more colorful salad.

> **Escarole Apple Bacon Salad:** Top escarole with apple, blue cheese, cooked bacon and walnuts.

# Greek Salad Skewers

Let's call this what it is—Greek salad on a stick! Easy to make ahead of time, these skewers are colorful, fun to serve, and full of flavor from the homemade Italian dressing. They work as a naturally gluten-free appetizer all by themselves, or you could pair them with grilled pita triangles.

**SEASON:**
Summer, fall

**VEGETARIAN**

**Makes 36 skewers | Prep time: 5 minutes, plus 2 hours to overnight to marinate**

1 pint grape tomatoes, halved

1 large English cucumber, cut into quarters

1 (9.5-ounce) jar pitted kalamata olives, drained

1½ cups prepared Italian Dressing (page 99), divided

1 (8-ounce) block of feta cheese, cut into 36 cubes

1. In a large bowl, combine the tomatoes, cucumber, and olives. Add 1 cup of Italian dressing and toss to combine. Cover and refrigerate for at least 2 hours or overnight.

2. Put the feta cubes in a separate small bowl. Add the remaining ½ cup of Italian dressing and toss to combine. Cover and refrigerate for at least 2 hours or overnight.

3. To assemble, layer an olive, tomato, cucumber, and then a feta cube onto each skewer. Serve immediately.

**PER SERVING (6 SKEWERS):**
Calories: 283; Total fat: 23g; Carbohydrates: 14g; Fiber: 2g; Protein: 7g; Calcium: 240mg; Vitamin D: 6mcg; Vitamin $B_{12}$: 0mcg; Iron: 2mg; Zinc: 1mg

➤ **Make it easier:** If the grape tomatoes aren't too big, keep them whole to save time.

**VARIATIONS:**

➤ **Chopped Greek Salad:** Ditch the skewers and toss the ingredients in a bowl for a more traditional Greek Salad.

➤ **Greek Pasta Salad:** Toss all the ingredients together with cooked whole-wheat pasta for a Greek twist on pasta salad.

# Grilled Romaine Caesar Salad

This is not your run-of-the-mill Caesar salad. Grilling romaine takes things up a notch by softening the ribs and slightly charring the leaves, adding a depth of flavor. The homemade dressing may take more effort than opening a store-bought bottle, but it's well worth it.

**Serves 4 | Prep time: 15 minutes | Cook time: 5 minutes**

## FOR THE DRESSING

½ cup plain Greek yogurt

½ lemon, juiced

2 teaspoons olive oil

2 teaspoons white wine
   vinegar

2 teaspoons Dijon mustard

1 teaspoon anchovy paste

½ teaspoon garlic powder

¼ cup grated Parmesan cheese

Salt

Freshly ground black pepper

## FOR THE SALAD

1 tablespoon canola oil

2 romaine hearts, cut in
   half lengthwise

½ cup herb-seasoned
   croutons

2 tablespoons grated
   Parmesan cheese

1. **To make the dressing:** In a bowl, stir together the yogurt, lemon juice, olive oil, vinegar, Dijon, anchovy paste, garlic powder, and Parmesan cheese. Season with salt and pepper to taste. Cover and refrigerate until ready to use.

2. **To make the salad:** Preheat the grill to medium-high heat. Brush the grill grates with the canola oil.

3. Place the romaine hearts cut-side down on the grill, and cook for about 3 minutes, or until they have developed grill marks.

4. Flip the romaine hearts grilled-side up. Drizzle with the dressing, and top with croutons and Parmesan cheese.

➤ **Prep tip:** Keep the romaine core intact when slicing, so the leaves stay together on the grill.

**VARIATIONS:**

➢ **Warm Kale Caesar Salad:** Sauté 1 bunch of kale in a sauté pan or skillet with 2 tablespoons of olive oil, until just wilted. Top with croutons, Parmesan, and Caesar dressing.

➢ **Grilled Romaine Cobb Salad:** Ditch the croutons, Parmesan, and Caesar dressing in favor of chopped tomato, hard-boiled egg, chopped bacon, and blue cheese.

**PER SERVING:** Calories: 155; Total fat: 10g; Carbohydrates: 11g; Fiber: 4g; Protein: 6g; Calcium: 171mg; Vitamin D: 3mcg; Vitamin B$_{12}$: 0mcg; Iron: 2mg; Zinc: 1mg

# Mediterranean Salad with Crispy Artichokes and Potatoes

SEASON:
Spring, summer, fall, winter

**VEGETARIAN**

This salad hits the mark on flavor, texture, and nutrition. The crispy artichokes, roasted potatoes, and sliced almonds add crunch and depth, while the arugula, tomatoes, and olives offer a mix of spicy, sweet, and salty. This one stands on its own as a meal, or you can give it a boost with a favorite protein, such as grilled shrimp or chicken.

**Serves 4 to 6 | Prep time: 10 minutes | Cook time: 15 to 18 minutes**

2 tablespoons olive oil

2 Yukon Gold potatoes, diced

1 teaspoon salt

½ teaspoon freshly ground black pepper

1 (12-ounce) jar marinated artichokes, drained and quartered

¼ cup mayonnaise

2 tablespoons white wine vinegar

1 teaspoon smoked paprika

½ teaspoon cayenne pepper

4 to 6 ounces arugula

6 ounces grape or cherry tomatoes, halved

1 cup green olives, pitted and sliced

4 ounces crumbled feta cheese

¼ cup sliced almonds

1. Heat the olive oil in a large sauté pan or skillet over medium heat. Add the potatoes, along with salt and black pepper, tossing occasionally for 10 minutes, or until crispy. Transfer the potatoes to a plate lined with a paper towel.

2. Put the artichoke hearts in the same pan and cook 5 to 7 minutes, until crispy, flipping once.

3. While the artichokes are cooking, whisk together the mayonnaise, vinegar, paprika, and cayenne pepper in a small bowl.

4. To serve, divide the arugula onto plates, along with the tomatoes and olives. Top with the potatoes, artichokes, crumbled feta, and sliced almonds. Drizzle with the dressing and enjoy.

➢ **Beyond the basics:** Instead of jarred artichokes, grab a whole fresh artichoke from the produce section. Trim off the outer leaves, remove the fuzzy choke and stem, and quarter it to panfry until crispy.

## VARIATIONS:

➢ **Fall Harvest Mediterranean Salad:** Swap the arugula for kale and the potatoes for roasted butternut squash for a sweeter option.

➢ **Mediterranean Green Bean Salad:** Try crunchy green beans in place of panfried artichoke hearts over your choice of lettuce greens.

**PER SERVING:** Calories: 498; Total fat: 30g; Carbohydrates: 48g; Fiber: 13g; Protein: 13g; Calcium: 275mg; Vitamin D: 5mcg; Vitamin B$_{12}$: 1mcg; Iron: 4mg; Zinc: 2mg

# Root-to-Stem Rainbow Salad with Easy Herb Vinaigrette

SEASON:
Spring, summer, fall, winter

VEGAN

This salad uses plant roots, stems, and everything in between. The addition of leaves, flowers, fruits, and seeds builds a beautifully colorful dish that opens up a conversation about food. Start with the basic colors of red, orange, yellow, green, blue, and purple using a variety of plant parts. Once you've got the basics down, add in more of your favorite vegetables and taste the rainbow.

**Serves 4 to 6 | Prep time: 10 minutes**

3 cups fresh baby spinach

1 small head radicchio, chopped coarsely

3 carrots, shredded

1 bunch asparagus, chopped

2 cups chopped purple cauliflower florets

1 cup halved cherry tomatoes

1 cup corn kernels

2 tablespoons white wine vinegar

2 tablespoons olive oil

1 tablespoon lemon juice

1 teaspoon Dijon mustard

1 teaspoon garlic powder

1 teaspoon dried oregano

1. In a large bowl, combine the baby spinach and the radicchio, then add in the carrots, asparagus, cauliflower, tomatoes, and corn, tossing to mix.

2. In a mason jar or a small container with a lid, combine the vinegar, olive oil, lemon juice, mustard, garlic powder, and oregano. Shake well.

3. Pour the dressing over the salad to serve. The dressing keeps well in the refrigerator for up to 1 week, but be sure to shake it well before using.

➤ **Prep tip:** Switch up the plant parts for a unique salad each time you make it. Here are some suggestions to get you started: **Roots** (carrot, radish); **Stems** (asparagus, celery); **Leaves** (lettuce, cabbage, celery leaves, spinach, Swiss chard, kale); **Flowers** (broccoli, cauliflower); **Fruits** (avocado, cucumber, pepper, tomato); **Seeds** (corn, peas).

## VARIATIONS:

➤ **Rainbow Skewers:** Build a rainbow salad on a stick by stacking red cherry tomatoes, orange wedges, yellow bell peppers, green cucumber slices, and blueberries. Serve with a creamy dip like the Greek yogurt dressing from the Sweet and Spicy Citrus Salad (page 85).

➤ **Roasted Rainbow Veggies on a Sheet Pan:** Preheat the oven to 375°F. Toss the tomatoes, carrots, corn, kale, and cauliflower with olive oil, salt, and pepper, and spread them out evenly on a sheet pan. Roast for 25 to 30 minutes, or until crispy and fork-tender.

**PER SERVING:** Calories: 168; Total fat: 8g; Carbohydrates: 24g; Fiber: 6g; Protein: 6g; Calcium: 82mg; Vitamin D: 0mcg; Vitamin B$_{12}$: 0mcg; Iron: 3mg; Zinc: 1mg

# Roasted Vegetable Salad with Goat Cheese

SEASON:
Fall, winter

**VEGETARIAN**

This salad is so full of flavor that it doesn't even need dressing. Kale, when well massaged, will convert even the biggest skeptic, especially when it's topped with roasted squash, Brussels sprouts, root vegetables, and creamy goat cheese.

**Serves 4 to 6 | Prep time: 15 minutes | Cook time: 25 minutes**

2 cups peeled and cubed
  butternut squash
½ pound Brussels
  sprouts, halved
2 medium carrots, chopped
  into 2-inch pieces
1 rutabaga, peeled and cubed
¼ cup olive oil, plus more
  for drizzling
1 teaspoon salt
½ teaspoon freshly ground
  black pepper
2 bunches kale, stemmed
  and chopped
4 ounces goat cheese
¼ cup roasted pumpkin seeds
  (see the vegetable profile,
  page 47)
¼ cup dried cranberries

**PER SERVING:** Calories: 413;
Total fat: 25g; Carbohydrates: 41g;
Fiber: 11g; Protein: 16g;
Calcium: 305mg; Vitamin D: 4mcg;
Vitamin B$_{12}$: 0mcg; Iron: 5mg;
Zinc: 2mg

1. Preheat the oven to 375°F.
2. Toss the butternut squash, Brussels sprouts, carrots, and rutabaga with olive oil and season with salt and pepper. Divide evenly between 2 sheet pans, spreading the pieces out to give the veggies space.
3. Roast for 20 to 25 minutes, until fork-tender. Remove the pans from the oven and allow the vegetables to cool for 2 to 3 minutes.
4. While the vegetables are roasting, drizzle the kale with olive oil and massage it thoroughly to soften.
5. To serve, toss the roasted vegetables with the kale, then crumble goat cheese on top and sprinkle with pumpkin seeds and dried cranberries.

**VARIATIONS:**

➤ **Roasted Root Salad:** Skip the Brussels sprouts and add in any root veggies you can find (beets, parsnips, or turnips would be delicious).
➤ **Summer Grilled Vegetable Salad:** Replace the roasted root vegetables with your favorite grilled summer veggies (corn and zucchini are some of mine), and serve over a bed of spinach instead of kale.

# Italian Chopped Salad

SEASON:
Spring, summer, fall

**VEGETARIAN**

Antipasto, served as a traditional first course in Italian culture, was the inspiration behind this veggie-filled chopped salad. Of course, it can be served before a pasta entrée, or it can hold its own as a meal itself. Either way, *mangia*!

**Serves 4 | Prep time: 20 minutes**

### FOR THE ITALIAN DRESSING

3 tablespoons red wine vinegar

2 garlic cloves, finely minced

1 teaspoon sugar

½ teaspoon dried oregano

½ teaspoon dried basil

½ teaspoon salt

¼ teaspoon freshly ground black pepper

⅓ cup olive oil

### FOR THE SALAD

2 heads romaine lettuce, chopped

1 yellow bell pepper, chopped

1 cup halved grape tomatoes

¼ cup stemmed and chopped pepperoncini

1 (6-ounce) jar artichoke hearts, drained and chopped

¼ cup thinly sliced red onion

½ cup mozzarella pearls

1. **To make the dressing:** In a small mason jar, combine the red wine vinegar, garlic, sugar, oregano, basil, salt, black pepper, and olive oil. Close the lid and shake until well mixed. Alternatively, whisk the ingredients in a bowl to combine.

2. **To make the salad:** In a large bowl, combine the romaine, bell pepper, tomatoes, pepperoncini, artichoke hearts, red onion, and mozzarella pearls. Drizzle with the dressing and toss together.

➤ **Beyond the basics:** Practice your knife skills (see page 16) by purchasing fresh artichokes to get the artichoke hearts for this chopped salad.

### VARIATIONS:

➤ **Italian Salad Skewers:** Stack the romaine, peppers, tomatoes, pepperoncini, artichoke hearts, red onion, and mozzarella on a skewer, and serve the dressing on the side as a dip.

➤ **Mediterranean Chopped Salad:** Sub the pepperoncini for cucumber and mozzarella for feta to change up the flavor profile.

**PER SERVING:** Calories: 303; Total fat: 22g; Carbohydrates: 22g; Fiber: 11g; Protein: 9g; Calcium: 201mg; Vitamin D: 2mcg; Vitamin B$_{12}$: 0mcg; Iron: 4mg; Zinc: 1mg

# Cooled Cucumber-Avocado Soup

**VEGETARIAN**

Move over, gazpacho. This creamy, cool summer soup is ready to show off all those garden cukes, especially on the nights when it's just too hot to turn on the stove. Top with extra diced avocado, cucumber, or even bell peppers for added texture and flavor.

**Serves 4 to 6 | Prep time: 10 minutes**

2 cucumbers, roughly chopped

½ onion

2 avocados, pitted

½ cup plain, full-fat
   Greek yogurt

2 teaspoons lime juice

Salt

Freshly ground black pepper

2 tablespoons chopped chives

**PER SERVING:** Calories: 230; Total fat: 16g; Carbohydrates: 20g; Fiber: 10g; Protein: 6g; Calcium: 81mg; Vitamin D: 1mcg; Vitamin B$_{12}$: 0mcg; Iron: 1mg; Zinc: 1mg

1. In a blender or food processor, combine the cucumbers, onion, avocado, Greek yogurt, lime juice, salt, and pepper. Puree until smooth.

2. Divide into bowls and serve with a garnish of chopped chives.

➤ **Prep tip:** This soup benefits from chilling in the refrigerator before serving. If you have the time, refrigerate for a few hours or overnight.

## VARIATIONS:

➤ **Spicy Cucumber-Avocado Soup:** Add a jalapeño pepper to the mix for some heat to balance out the coolness of the cucumber.

➤ **Celery Soup:** Replace the cucumbers with 3 or 4 celery stalks (and leaves) and garnish with extra diced celery for crunch.

# Summer Squash Soup

SEASON:
Summer

VEGAN

Summer squash always seems to be picked over for its cousin the zucchini, but this soup may just change all that with its light and refreshing flavor that becomes even brighter with fresh basil. The yellow color of summer squash indicates that it is high in vitamin A, or more specifically, beta carotene, a carotenoid that acts like an antioxidant.

**Serves 4 to 6 | Prep time: 5 minutes | Cook time: 25 minutes**

2 tablespoons olive oil

1 small onion, diced

4 yellow squash, chopped

2 celery stalks, diced

1 teaspoon salt

¼ teaspoon freshly ground black pepper

4 cups vegetable broth

2 tablespoons lemon juice

¼ cup chopped fresh basil

**PER SERVING:** Calories: 113; Total fat: 7g; Carbohydrates: 12g; Fiber: 3g; Protein: 3g; Calcium: 40mg; Vitamin D: 0mcg; Vitamin B$_{12}$: 0mcg; Iron: 1mg; Zinc: 1mg

1. In a large pot, heat the olive oil over medium heat and add the onion, cooking for 2 to 3 minutes, or until soft.

2. Add the squash and celery, and season with salt and pepper. Stir and cook for 5 minutes.

3. Add the broth and lemon juice. Bring to a boil, then reduce the heat and simmer for about 10 minutes.

4. Transfer to a blender or use an immersion blender to puree the soup. Divide the soup into bowls to serve, and garnish with basil.

➢ **Prep tip:** When chopping the celery, keep the leaves on to add some depth and a stronger celery flavor to the soup.

**VARIATIONS:**

➢ **Creamy Summer Squash Soup:** Add a ½ cup of buttermilk or coconut milk to the mixture before pureeing for a thicker, creamier soup.

➢ **Asparagus Soup:** Trade out the summer squash for 2 bunches of spring asparagus and add ¼ cup of grated Parmesan.

# Lemony Lentil-Turnip Soup

SEASON:
Fall, winter, spring

**VEGETARIAN**

Simple ingredients, good quality nutrition, and lots of flavor—what more can you ask from a soup? One serving of this bold-colored lentil soup boasts almost 10 grams of protein and is sure to warm you up. It also helps fight inflammation with citrus, turmeric, and other spices.

**Serves 6 | Prep time: 10 minutes | Cook time: 35 minutes**

2 tablespoons olive oil

1 small onion, chopped

½ cup chopped celery

4 garlic cloves, minced

1 teaspoon turmeric

1 teaspoon ground cumin

½ teaspoon salt

¼ teaspoon freshly ground
    black pepper

1 cup peeled and
    chopped turnips

1 cup red lentils

1 lemon, zested and juiced

6 cups water

Chopped fresh parsley,
    for garnish

**PER SERVING:** Calories: 174; Total fat: 5g; Carbohydrates: 25g; Fiber: 4g; Protein: 8g; Calcium: 36mg; Vitamin D: 0mcg; Vitamin $B_{12}$: 0mcg; Iron: 3mg; Zinc: 1mg

1. Heat the olive oil in a large pot over medium-high. Add the onion and celery, and cook until the onions are soft and translucent. Add garlic and stir for 1 minute more, or until fragrant.

2. Add the turmeric, cumin, salt, and pepper. Stir to combine. Add the turnips, lentils, lemon zest, and water. Bring to a boil, then reduce the heat to a simmer for 20 to 25 minutes, until turnips are fork-tender and the lentils are cooked through. Add more water, if needed.

3. Stir in the lemon juice. Serve and garnish with parsley.

➤ **Make it easier:** Cut back on prep time by purchasing premade mirepoix, a mixture of diced onions, carrots, and celery, to use in this and other soups.

**VARIATIONS:**

➤ **Lemony Lentil Soup with Kale:** Stir 1 cup of loosely chopped kale into the soup when adding the lemon juice.
➤ **Lemony Turnip-Corn Soup:** Don't have lentils? Sub in frozen corn kernels for more sweetness.

# Simple Ratatouille Soup

SEASON:
Summer

**VEGETARIAN**

A traditional, chunky French stew, ratatouille is usually served more as a casserole dish, but this soup version is a tasty and easy way to use up lots of summer vegetables, like tomatoes and zucchini, at once. The creamy and tangy goat cheese garnish takes things up a notch by offsetting the natural sweetness of the veggies. Bon appétit!

**Serves 4 to 6 | Prep time: 10 minutes | Cook time: 35 minutes**

2 tablespoons olive oil

2 garlic cloves, minced

1 medium onion, diced

1 medium eggplant, peeled and cubed

2 medium zucchini, chopped

2 sweet bell peppers, chopped

1 (28-ounce) can crushed tomatoes

1 teaspoon dried rosemary

½ teaspoon dried thyme

½ teaspoon salt

¼ teaspoon freshly ground black pepper

4 cups vegetable broth

4 ounces goat cheese, for garnish

---

**PER SERVING:** Calories: 268; Total fat: 14g; Carbohydrates: 30g; Fiber: 10g; Protein: 11g; Calcium: 157mg; Vitamin D: 4mcg; Vitamin B$_{12}$: 0mcg; Iron: 3mg; Zinc: 1mg

1. Heat the olive oil in a large pot over medium heat. Add the garlic and onions, and cook for 2 to 3 minutes, or until the onions are soft and translucent.

2. Add the eggplant, zucchini, bell peppers, crushed tomatoes, rosemary, thyme, salt, and black pepper. Cook for approximately 5 minutes, stirring occasionally.

3. Add the broth and bring it to a boil, then reduce the heat and simmer for 20 minutes.

4. When ready to serve, top with a small spoonful of creamy goat cheese as a garnish.

---

## VARIATIONS:

➤ **Roasted Vegetable Ratatouille Soup:** Put the eggplant, zucchini, and bell peppers on a sheet pan, drizzle with the olive oil, and roast for about 30 minutes. Add the roasted veggies to the soup mixture, bring to a boil, and simmer for about 10 minutes.

➤ **Ratatouille Salad:** Ditch the broth and crushed tomatoes, and serve the sautéed, seasoned vegetables over a bed of greens with sliced tomatoes.

# Mushroom-Kale Soup with White Beans and Farro

SEASON:
Winter

**VEGAN**

Ready for a big bowl of feel-good food? Grated or shredded potato adds a unique thickness to this veggie-packed soup. Mushrooms offer up vitamin D and $B_{12}$, while the kale provides vitamin A and C, plus fiber to boot.

**Serves 8 | Prep time: 10 minutes | Cook time: 25 minutes**

2 tablespoons olive oil

2 garlic cloves

1 medium onion, chopped

2 celery stalks, minced

8 ounces button mushrooms, sliced

8 cups vegetable broth

1 (15-ounce) can white beans, drained and rinsed

½ cup dry farro

2 teaspoons dried thyme

1 teaspoon dried oregano

1 teaspoon dried basil

1 bunch kale, stemmed and chopped (about 2 cups)

1 medium potato, peeled and shredded

**PER SERVING:** Calories: 162; Total fat: 4g; Carbohydrates: 27g; Fiber: 5g; Protein: 7g; Calcium: 77mg; Vitamin D: 2mcg; Vitamin $B_{12}$: 0mcg; Iron: 2mg; Zinc: 1mg

1. Heat the olive oil in a large stockpot over medium heat. Add the garlic, onion, and celery and sauté for 2 to 3 minutes. Stir in the mushrooms, cooking until golden brown.

2. Pour the vegetable broth, beans, farro, thyme, oregano, and basil into the mushroom mixture and bring to a boil, then reduce to a simmer.

3. After 15 minutes, stir in the chopped kale and shredded potato. Continue to cook until the farro is tender, approximately 10 minutes.

➤ **Beyond the basics:** Because you'll have a lot more veggies around, cut back on waste and use the scraps and leftovers to make a DIY vegetable broth (see page 15).

**VARIATIONS:**

➤ **Collard and Lentil Soup:** Collard greens and lentils fit nicely in place of the kale and white beans.

➤ **Black Bean and Kale Tortilla Soup:** Substitute corn and black beans for the mushrooms and white beans. Add jalapeños, swap the spices for cilantro, stir in tortilla strips and add chicken, if desired.

# Veggie-Loaded Potato Soup with Bacon

SEASON:
Winter

**VEGETARIAN OPTION**
(see headnote)

This soup has all the yumminess of a loaded, creamy, cheesy baked potato—but isn't as heavy. Skip the bacon and add a little extra butter for a vegetarian version, and serve with endless options of garnishes and toppings.

**Serves 4 to 6 | Prep time: 5 minutes | Cook time: 40 minutes**

6 slices bacon

3 tablespoons butter, divided

1 medium onion, diced

2 garlic cloves, minced

2 medium russet
 potatoes, chopped

8 cups vegetable broth

2 cups chopped broccoli,
 stems and florets

1 cup shredded carrots

1 leek, chopped

¼ cup flour

1 cup whole milk

2 cups shredded cheddar, plus
 more (optional) for garnish

Fresh chives, for
 garnish (optional)

Sour cream, for
 garnish (optional)

---

**PER SERVING:** Calories: 613;
Total fat: 36g; Carbohydrates: 47g;
Fiber: 4g; Protein: 27g;
Calcium: 522mg; Vitamin D: 24mcg;
Vitamin B$_{12}$: 1mcg; Iron: 3mg;
Zinc: 3mg

1. In a large skillet or sauté pan, cook the bacon over medium heat until the fat renders, 10 to 12 minutes, flipping halfway through. Put the bacon on a plate lined with paper towels, allow it to cool, then crumble. Reserve some of the bacon fat.

2. In a large stockpot or Dutch oven, melt 2 tablespoons of butter and the bacon fat, add in the onion and garlic, and cook them for 2 to 3 minutes, until aromatic.

3. Add the potatoes and broth, bring to a boil, then cover and simmer for 10 minutes.

4. Add the broccoli, shredded carrots, and leek and continue to simmer for 15 minutes.

5. In the skillet used to cook the bacon, whisk 1 tablespoon of butter and the flour together until it begins to brown. Pour in the milk, constantly whisking, then add in the cheddar to melt. Stir the cheese sauce into the pot or Dutch oven, and simmer for 5 more minutes.

6. Top with crumbled bacon and optional toppings such as chives, sour cream, and additional cheddar, if desired.

➤ **Make it easier:** Use pre-shredded hash browns or tater tots in place of chopped potatoes.

**VARIATIONS:**

➤ **Sweet Potato Soup with Bacon and Broccoli:**
Replace russet potatoes with sweet potatoes for a
sweeter soup.

➤ **Cauliflower Potato Soup with Bacon:** Swap out the
broccoli for cauliflower for a less colorful—but just as
nutritious and delicious—soup option.

Spaghetti Squash Burrito Bowls, 121

# CHAPTER 6

# Vegetable Mains

# Apple, Cheddar, and Collard Wraps

SEASON:
Fall, winter

**VEGETARIAN**

Inspired by one of my favorite sandwich picks at a national fast-casual restaurant chain, this sandwich combines fruits and vegetables with walnuts and cheese all bundled up in a collard wrap. The size and texture of collard greens make them a perfect sub for wraps and tortillas, but you can also stick to a traditional wrap and stuff the collard greens inside.

**Serves 4 | Prep time: 10 minutes**

¼ head cabbage, chopped

1 apple, chopped

½ tablespoon apple
   cider vinegar

2 tablespoons lemon juice

1 tablespoon honey

½ cup dried cranberries

½ cup chopped walnuts

4 large collard green leaves

6 slices mild cheddar cheese

---

**PER SERVING:** Calories: 382;
Total fat: 24g; Carbohydrates: 32g;
Fiber: 6g; Protein: 14g;
Calcium: 424mg; Vitamin D: 17mcg;
Vitamin $B_{12}$: 0mcg; Iron: 1mg;
Zinc: 2mg

1. In a large bowl, combine the cabbage, chopped apple, apple cider vinegar, lemon juice, honey, dried cranberries, and walnuts.

2. Before preparing the sandwiches, trim the stems from the collard green leaves and blanch each for about 1 minute in a pan filled with ½ inch of boiling water (see blanching tips on page 19). Remove the leaves from the pan, dip in an ice bath, and pat dry.

3. To assemble the sandwiches, lay 1½ slices of cheddar cheese on each collard green leaf, then scoop approximately ¾ cup of the slaw mixture into the wrap. Fold the short ends of the leaf inward and roll lengthwise. Cut in half and serve.

➤ **Prep tip:** Blanch an entire bunch of collard greens at one time, layer parchment paper between the leaves, and put them in a large zip-top bag to store in the refrigerator for up to 1 week.

➤ **Autumn Roasted Vegetable Wraps:** Sub your favorite roasted fall veggies (think butternut squash, Brussels sprouts, or sweet potatoes) for the cabbage and wrap it all up in a large kale leaf.

➤ **Apple, Cheddar, and Spinach Salad:** Serve the apple and cabbage mixture over a bed of baby spinach with shredded cheddar cheese.

# Spiced Cauliflower and Chickpea Tacos

SEASON:
Spring, summer, fall, winter

**VEGETARIAN**

Consider these tacos your new favorite way to enjoy cauliflower, the cruciferous veggie that packs a punch with plenty of vitamins C and K, potassium, folate, and fiber. Enjoy the tacos as they are, and be sure to save any leftover filling to serve again as a side dish.

**Serves 4 to 6 | Prep time: 5 minutes | Cook time: 35 minutes**

1 head cauliflower, chopped into florets

1 (15-ounce) can chickpeas, drained and rinsed

4 tablespoons olive oil

½ teaspoon garlic powder

½ teaspoon onion powder

1½ teaspoons chili powder

½ teaspoon ground cumin

½ head red cabbage, chopped

¾ cup plain Greek yogurt

¼ cup chopped fresh cilantro

2 tablespoons lime juice

12 corn tortillas

**PER SERVING:** Calories: 450; Total fat: 19g; Carbohydrates: 62g; Fiber: 13g; Protein: 14g; Calcium: 212mg; Vitamin D: 1mcg; Vitamin $B_{12}$: 0mcg; Iron: 3mg; Zinc: 2mg

1. Preheat the oven to 400°F. Combine the cauliflower and chickpeas in a large bowl. Add the olive oil, garlic powder, onion powder, chili powder, and ground cumin. Toss or stir to evenly coat, then pour the mixture onto a sheet pan.

2. Roast in the oven for 30 to 35 minutes, or until the cauliflower begins to brown and the chickpeas become crunchy.

3. While the cauliflower and chickpeas are roasting, mix the red cabbage, Greek yogurt, cilantro, and lime juice in a medium bowl until the cabbage is well coated.

4. To serve, place a large spoonful of cabbage slaw on each tortilla and top with the roasted cauliflower and chickpea mixture.

➤ **Make it easier:** There's no shame in a frozen food game here. Use frozen cauliflower florets and thaw before combining with chickpeas to roast.

**VARIATIONS:**

➤ **Spiced Cauliflower and Chickpea Enchiladas:** Use the cauliflower chickpea mixture to stuff tortillas, then line a casserole dish, top with enchilada sauce and cheese, and bake for 20 minutes at 375°F.

➤ **Broccoli and Black Bean Tacos:** Replace the cauliflower and chickpeas with broccoli and black beans for a comparable and nutritious dish.

# Bok Choy, Lentil, and Quinoa Bowls with Quick-Pickled Radishes

SEASON:
Winter

**VEGAN**

Bok choy used to be intimidating to me, until I learned how easy it is to cook. Now it's a go-to vegetable for nights when I want to jazz up a dish using inexpensive staples like lentils and quinoa. The quick-pickled radishes add spice and crunch to an otherwise soft, mellow dish.

**Serves 4 | Prep time: 5 minutes | Cook time: 35 minutes**

¾ cup lentils

4 cups low-sodium vegetable broth

4 radishes, thinly sliced

2 to 3 tablespoons white wine vinegar

2 tablespoons olive oil

1 garlic clove, minced

8 ounces mushrooms, sliced

1 tablespoon ground ginger

4 baby bok choy, leaves separated and stems chopped

1 tablespoon soy sauce

1 teaspoon salt

½ teaspoon freshly ground black pepper

1 cup quinoa

1. In a large pot or Dutch oven, bring the lentils and vegetable broth to a boil, then reduce the heat and simmer for 15 minutes.

2. While the lentils are cooking, put the sliced radishes in a small bowl with the white wine vinegar to marinate.

3. Heat the olive oil and garlic in a skillet or saucepan over medium heat, cooking 1 to 2 minutes, or until fragrant. Add the sliced mushrooms, ground ginger, baby bok choy, and soy sauce, and sauté for about 5 minutes. Season with salt and pepper.

4. While sautéing the vegetables, add the quinoa to the pot with the broth and lentils, then stir and continue to cook for 12 to 15 more minutes.

5. To serve, divide the quinoa and lentil mixture into bowls, top with the mushroom and bok choy mixture, and garnish with the pickled radishes.

➤ **Prep tip:** Make a larger batch of pickled radishes (or any pickled veggies, see page 20) in advance, and use to garnish.

## VARIATIONS:

➤ **Broccoli and Lentil Quinoa Bowl:** Use broccoli or rapini (broccoli rabe) in place of the bok choy if you're just getting into veggie dishes.

➤ **Bok Choy Noodle Bowl:** Add an extra 8 ounces of vegetable broth and replace quinoa with udon noodles for a veggie-filled noodle bowl.

**PER SERVING:** Calories: 391; Total fat: 10g; Carbohydrates: 60g; Fiber: 9g; Protein: 18g; Calcium: 61mg; Vitamin D: 4mcg; Vitamin $B_{12}$: 0mcg; Iron: 5mg; Zinc: 3mg

# Braised Mediterranean-Style Leeks

SEASON:
Fall, winter, spring

**VEGETARIAN**

Beyond potato leek soup, many people don't know what the heck to do with leeks. This dish is an easy and light way to show those leeks some love and impress your family at the same time. The chickpeas and feta bump up the protein and fat for a well-rounded meal, but you can also add fish or meat on the side.

**Serves 4 to 6 | Prep time: 5 minutes | Cook time: 10 minutes**

4 leeks

1½ cups vegetable broth

¼ cup olive oil

2 garlic cloves, minced

1 teaspoon honey

2 lemons, zested and juiced

½ teaspoon salt

½ teaspoon freshly ground
   black pepper

1 (15-ounce) can chickpeas,
   rinsed and drained

4 ounces feta
   cheese, crumbled

**PER SERVING:** Calories: 344; Total fat: 21g; Carbohydrates: 32g; Fiber: 5g; Protein: 10g; Calcium: 221mg; Vitamin D: 5mcg; Vitamin B$_{12}$: 0mcg; Iron: 3mg; Zinc: 1mg

1. Slice off the root end of the leeks, and slice them in half lengthwise. Rinse well between the layers to remove any dirt.

2. Cut the stalks into 1-inch sections diagonally. Use the white and pale green portions, discarding the darkest part or repurposing it for stocks/soups.

3. In a large saucepan, heat the vegetable broth over medium-high heat until it simmers. Put the leeks in the simmering broth and cover for 5 to 10 minutes.

4. While the leeks are cooking, whisk together the olive oil, garlic, honey, lemon juice, salt, and pepper in a bowl.

5. Using tongs or a slotted spoon, add the cooked leeks to the bowl, then toss them in the dressing. Discard the broth or save and reuse for other recipes.

6. Add the chickpeas and feta to the leek mixture and serve topped with lemon zest.

➤ **Prep tip:** When juicing a fresh lemon, slice in half and squeeze with the cut-side up to prevent seeds from falling down into the bowl.

---

## VARIATIONS:

➤ **Braised Mediterranean-Style Celery:** Swap the leeks with sliced celery, and serve your favorite meat or fish on top.

➤ **Lemony Leeks and Carrots with Parmesan:** Replace 2 of the leeks with 2 medium carrots, cut in half lengthwise, and swap the feta with Parmesan.

# Cauliflower Crust Pizza

SEASON:
Fall, winter

**VEGETARIAN**

As a New Yorker, I will be the first to say that cauliflower pizza cannot and does not take the place of flour-based pizza crust. Rather than think of this as a carb alternative, think of it as a new, fun way to enjoy more cruciferous veggies. It took some trial and error, but this pizza has a crispy cauliflower crust that's full of flavor. Do yourself a favor and use a store-bought riced cauliflower to make the crust, unless you have a food processor or ricer.

**Serves 4 | Prep time: 15 minutes | Cook time: 30 minutes**

## FOR THE CRUST

4 cups riced cauliflower

¾ cup shredded mozzarella

½ cup grated Parmesan

2 large eggs

1 tablespoon Italian seasoning

¼ teaspoon salt

## FOR THE TOPPINGS

1 cup Simple Marinara Sauce (page 185) or store-bought

2 cups shredded mozzarella

½ cup chopped fresh basil

**PER SERVING:** Calories: 361; Total fat: g; Carbohydrates: 12g; Fiber: 3g; Protein: 27g; Calcium: 457mg; Vitamin D: 35mcg; Vitamin $B_{12}$: 2mcg; Iron: 2mg; Zinc: 4mg

1. Preheat the oven to 425°F. Line a large sheet pan with parchment paper.

2. **To make the crust:** Pour the riced cauliflower in a microwave-safe dish. Microwave it uncovered for 10 minutes, stirring halfway through. Let cool. Stir the mozzarella, Parmesan, eggs, Italian seasoning, and salt into the riced cauliflower, and mix until well combined. Form the cauliflower mixture into one large circle or two smaller circles, pressing to approximately ¼-inch thickness. Bake until edges are browned and the center of the crust is firm, about 20 minutes.

3. **To make the toppings:** Remove the crusts from the oven and top them with tomato sauce and cheese. Bake 10 minutes more, or until the cheese has melted.

4. Remove them from the oven, and top with fresh basil.

➤ **Prep tip:** When adding the toppings, be sure to cook any vegetables first to prevent a soggy crust. For an extra crispy crust, flip it and bake 5 minutes more before adding toppings.

**VARIATIONS:**

➤ **Broccoli Crust Pizza:** Swap in riced broccoli for a different cruciferous veggie pizza crust.

➤ **Spinach Pesto Cauliflower Crust Pizza:** Take this pizza up a notch with a spinach and basil pesto sauce instead of marinara.

# Broccoli, Lemon, and White Bean Pasta

SEASON:
Summer, fall

**VEGETARIAN**

When life gives you lemons (and broccoli and spinach), make this pasta! Lemon juice brightens up this fiber-filled pasta dish, and it's ready in under 20 minutes.

**Serves 4 to 6 | Prep time: 5 minutes | Cook time: 15 minutes**

1 pound whole-wheat fusilli

1 head broccoli, chopped (4 to 5 cups)

3 tablespoons olive oil

1 (15-ounce) can white beans, drained and rinsed

2 cups spinach

1 teaspoon garlic powder

1 teaspoon red pepper flakes

Salt

Freshly ground black pepper

Juice from 2 lemons

Half a lemon, thinly sliced, for garnish

**PER SERVING:** Calories: 622; Total fat: 13g; Carbohydrates: 111g; Fiber: 19g; Protein: 26g; Calcium: 154mg; Vitamin D: 0mcg; Vitamin B$_{12}$: 0mcg; Iron: 7mg; Zinc: 4mg

1. Bring salted water to boil in a large pot. Cook the pasta for 7 to 8 minutes, then add the chopped broccoli and cook for 3 to 4 more minutes. Drain and return the pasta and broccoli to the pot.

2. Add the olive oil, white beans, and spinach, stirring until the spinach wilts.

3. Sprinkle in garlic powder, red pepper flakes, and salt and black pepper to taste.

4. Toss with the lemon juice and garnish with lemon slices to serve.

➤ **Beyond the basics:** Rather than adding in the broccoli as florets, consider making a broccoli pesto sauce by combining the olive oil, lemon juice, broccoli, garlic powder, and some pine nuts. Toss the pasta, white beans, and spinach together with the sauce and sprinkle with red pepper flakes.

**VARIATIONS:**

➤ **White Bean Pasta with Lemon and Arugula:** Omit the broccoli and stir in 4 cups of arugula in place of the spinach.

➤ **Tuscan Vegetable Pasta:** Use kale and sun-dried tomatoes to replace broccoli and spinach.

# Spaghetti Squash Burrito Bowls

SEASON:
Winter

**VEGETARIAN**

Who doesn't love a burrito bowl? If you want to look like an expert chef in front of friends and family, serve these burrito bowls the next time you have guests over. Served right inside the spaghetti squash, these bowls are colorful, fun, and delicious. Plus, they're packed with veggies and so darn easy to make.

**Serves 4 | Prep time: 15 minutes | Cook time: 50 minutes**

2 medium spaghetti squash

2 tablespoons olive oil, plus more for drizzling

½ teaspoon salt

¼ teaspoon freshly ground black pepper

1 medium onion, diced

1 bell pepper, diced

1 garlic clove, minced

1 (15-ounce) can corn, rinsed and drained

1 (15-ounce) can black beans, rinsed and drained

1 medium tomato, diced

1 tablespoon ground cumin

½ teaspoon ground cayenne pepper

6 ounces cheddar cheese, shredded

Cilantro, for garnish

1. Preheat the oven to 400°F and grease or line a sheet pan with parchment paper. Halve the spaghetti squash, then use a spoon to scoop out the seeds and discard them. Drizzle with olive oil and sprinkle with salt and black pepper. Place them cut-side down on the prepared sheet pan.

2. Roast in the oven for 45 to 50 minutes, or until a fork pierces the skin easily.

3. While the spaghetti squash is roasting, dice the onion and bell pepper.

4. Heat 2 tablespoons olive oil in a pan and add the garlic, onion, and bell pepper. Cook, stirring occasionally, until the peppers and onions begin to soften, about 5 minutes. Add in the corn, black beans, tomato, cumin, and cayenne pepper.

CONTINUED

5. When the spaghetti squash is done, allow it to cool before fluffing spaghetti strands with a fork. Distribute the black bean mixture into the squash halves, top with cheese, and return to the oven for 5 minutes more, or until the cheese is melted.

6. Garnish with chopped cilantro and serve with your preferred burrito fixings.

➤ **Prep tip:** If you're struggling to cut the spaghetti squash in half before roasting, pierce some holes in it with a fork and microwave for 3 to 4 minutes to soften the skin.

**VARIATIONS:**

➤ **Spinach and White Bean Stuffed Spaghetti Squash:** Sauté spinach with onions and garlic, adding in the white beans before filling the cooked spaghetti squash.

➤ **Greek Stuffed Spaghetti Squash:** Instead of cumin and cayenne, mellow out the flavor with dried basil and oregano, and add chickpeas and feta cheese in place of the black beans and cheddar for a Greek spin on this squash dish.

**PER SERVING:** Calories: 486; Total fat: 24g; Carbohydrates: 53g; Fiber: 13g; Protein: 21g; Calcium: 380mg; Vitamin D: 10mcg; Vitamin $B_{12}$: 0mcg; Iron: 4mg; Zinc: 3mg

# Broccoli-Cheddar Stuffed Potatoes

SEASON:
Fall, winter

**VEGETARIAN**

This is one of several stuffed vegetable recipes in this book. Broccoli and cheddar is a classic flavor combination that is showcased in a stuffed baked potato, a meal that is sure to please even the pickiest of eaters.

**Serves 4 | Prep time: 15 minutes | Cook time: 65 minutes**

4 medium russet potatoes

2 tablespoons butter

½ cup sour cream

3 tablespoons whole milk

½ teaspoon salt

¼ teaspoon freshly ground
   black pepper

½ teaspoon garlic powder

½ teaspoon onion powder

½ teaspoon paprika

1 cup cooked broccoli, cut into
   small florets

1 cup shredded sharp cheddar
   cheese, divided

1 teaspoon olive oil

**PER SERVING:** Calories: 423;
Total fat: 23g; Carbohydrates: 44g;
Fiber: 4g; Protein: 13g;
Calcium: 282mg; Vitamin D: 15mcg;
Vitamin B$_{12}$: 0mcg; Iron: 2mg;
Zinc: 2mg

1. Preheat the oven to 400°F. Line a sheet pan with parchment paper.

2. Pierce the potatoes with a fork and wrap each potato individually in aluminum foil. Bake them for 45 minutes, or until the potatoes are fork-tender.

3. Remove the potatoes from the foil and let them cool until they can be handled. Slice each potato in half lengthwise. Scoop out the white flesh from the potato into a bowl, being careful to keep the skins intact.

4. Add the butter to the bowl of potatoes and mash with a potato masher until smooth. Stir in the sour cream, whole milk, salt, pepper, garlic powder, onion powder, paprika, broccoli, and ¾ cup of cheese.

5. Using a pastry brush, brush the potato skins with olive oil and place them on the sheet pan. Divide the filling among the potato skins. Top with remaining cheddar cheese.

6. Bake for 20 minutes or until the cheese is melted and the potatoes are heated through.

CONTINUED

## Broccoli-Cheddar Stuffed Potatoes CONTINUED

> **Prep tip:** Stick a metal skewer directly through the potatoes before baking so they cook more consistently and quickly.

### VARIATIONS:

> **Southwest Stuffed Potatoes:** Swap out the broccoli and stuff the potatoes with sautéed peppers and onions.

> **Greek Stuffed Potatoes:** Replace broccoli and cheddar cheese with sun-dried tomatoes, artichokes, and feta.

# Carrot, Green Bean, and Tempeh Peanut Stir-Fry

SEASON: Spring, summer, fall, winter

**VEGAN**

Tempeh is my favorite plant-based protein, with a slightly nutty flavor and a chewier texture than tofu. The simple peanut stir-fry sauce is absorbed right into the tempeh and adds just the right amount of sweet and salty flavor to the veggies.

**Serves 4 to 6 | Prep time: 5 minutes | Cook time: 15 minutes**

2 tablespoons vegetable oil

2 (8-ounce) blocks tempeh, cubed

½ pound carrots, julienned

½ pound green beans

¼ cup low-sodium soy sauce

2 tablespoons apple cider vinegar

1 tablespoon creamy peanut butter

1 teaspoon brown sugar

½ teaspoon garlic powder

¼ teaspoon ground ginger

**PER SERVING:** Calories: 360; Total fat: 21g; Carbohydrates: 23g; Fiber: 4g; Protein: 25g; Calcium: 174mg; Vitamin D: 0mcg; Vitamin $B_{12}$: 0mcg; Iron: 4mg; Zinc: 2mg

1. Heat the oil in a pan, then add the tempeh and cook it for 2 to 3 minutes, flipping the cubes to crisp each side.

2. Add the carrots and green beans, cooking them 3 to 4 minutes more, or until they begin to brown slightly.

3. In a small bowl, whisk together soy sauce, vinegar, peanut butter, brown sugar, garlic powder, and ginger.

4. Pour the sauce over the tempeh and vegetables, reduce the heat, and simmer for 5 minutes.

➤ **Beyond the basics:** Marinate the tempeh cubes overnight, allowing the flavors to sink in, and bake at 350°F for 30 minutes for a crispy crunch.

**VARIATIONS:**

➤ **Broccoli and Bell Pepper Stir-Fry with Tempeh:** Use broccoli florets and sliced bell peppers in place of carrots and green beans, cooking the broccoli a few minutes longer to soften.

➤ **Balsamic Brussels Sprout Stir-Fry:** Replace the apple cider vinegar with balsamic vinegar and add sliced Brussels sprouts instead of carrots and green beans for a unique but tasty twist on this stir-fry.

# Fall Harvest Pizza

SEASON:
Fall

**VEGETARIAN**

Inspired by one of my favorite Trader Joe's frozen finds, which, sadly, has now been discontinued, this pizza is a cozy fall meal. I highly recommend advance planning with this one, so the next time you're roasting butternut squash and mashing sweet potatoes, you can add this pizza to your menu. With those ingredients ready to go, grab a store-bought pizza dough, and you'll have dinner on the table in 25 minutes.

**Serves 4 | Prep time: 10 minutes | Cook time: 15 minutes**

1 (16-ounce) package store-bought pizza dough

1 tablespoon olive oil

½ onion, sliced

1 cup mashed sweet potato

6 ounces butternut squash, roasted and chopped

2 ounces kale, chopped

4 ounces Parmesan cheese, thinly sliced

1 teaspoon salt

½ teaspoon freshly ground black pepper

**PER SERVING:** Calories: 518; Total fat: 15g; Carbohydrates: 79g; Fiber: 7g; Protein: 20g; Calcium: 331mg; Vitamin D: 6mcg; Vitamin B$_{12}$: 0mcg; Iron: 4mg; Zinc: 2mg

1. Preheat the oven to 425°F and allow the dough to sit out at room temperature.

2. While the oven is warming up, heat the olive oil in a pan and sauté the sliced onion until translucent.

3. Roll the dough out onto a sheet pan. Spread the mashed sweet potato evenly onto the dough.

4. Top the pizza with the onion, squash, kale, and Parmesan cheese. Season with salt and pepper.

5. Bake for 12 to 14 minutes, or until the crust is crisp.

➤ **Beyond the basics:** Take things up a notch in the kitchen and make your own pizza crust. May I suggest the cauliflower pizza crust on page 118?

## VARIATIONS:

➤ **Southwest Sweet Potato Pizza:** Instead of kale, butternut squash, and Parmesan, top the pizza with black beans, corn, tomatoes, and cheddar cheese.

➤ **Mediterranean Pizza:** For a more traditional veggie pizza pie, use tomato sauce and top with artichokes, olives, and goat cheese.

# Sweet Potato–Kale Frittata

SEASON:
Fall, winter

VEGETARIAN

This veggie-packed dish can be served for breakfast, lunch, or dinner and couldn't be easier to put together. Eggs are packed with protein and healthy fats, and the vegetables round out this meal with carbohydrates and fiber.

**Serves 4 | Prep time: 15 minutes | Cook time: 40 minutes**

1 tablespoon olive oil

1 large shallot, thinly sliced

2 cups stemmed and chopped kale

1 medium sweet potato, peeled, chopped, and steamed

½ teaspoon salt

¼ teaspoon freshly ground black pepper

10 large eggs

2 tablespoons goat cheese

**PER SERVING:** Calories: 252; Total fat: 16g; Carbohydrates: 9g; Fiber: 1g; Protein: 17g; Calcium: 98mg; Vitamin D: 103mcg; Vitamin B$_{12}$: 1mcg; Iron: 3mg; Zinc: 2mg

1. Preheat the oven to 425°F. Spray an 8-inch pie plate (or 8-by-8-inch square pan) with cooking spray.

2. In a large sauté pan or skillet, heat the olive oil over medium-high heat. Add the shallot slices and sauté until they begin to brown. Add the kale and a splash of water. Cover the pan with a lid. Allow steam to generate for about 1 minute. Remove the lid, then stir.

3. Add the sweet potatoes, salt, and pepper. Stir to combine.

4. In a large bowl, whisk the eggs.

5. Place the sautéed vegetables in an even layer in the prepared baking dish. Pour the eggs evenly over the vegetables. Sprinkle the goat cheese on top.

6. Bake for 35 to 40 minutes.

➤ **Prep tip:** Take time to whisk the eggs until light and frothy. This way they will rise better and be less dense after baking.

**VARIATIONS:**

➤ **Squash Frittata Bites:** Swap the sweet potatoes with butternut squash and bake in muffin tins instead of a pie plate.

➤ **Sweet Potato–Spinach Frittata:** You can also replace the kale with spinach or another leafy green.

# One-Pan Tuscan White Bean Skillet

SEASON:
Fall, winter

**VEGETARIAN**

When you think of comfort food, vegetables don't usually come to mind, but this one-pan skillet is here to change that. It's full of flavor, and it's a truly satisfying meal with an even more satisfying ending, meaning super-simple cleanup.

**Serves 4 | Prep time: 15 minutes | Cook time: 20 minutes**

1 tablespoon olive oil

1 large sweet onion, chopped

½ cup julienned sun-dried tomatoes

4 garlic cloves, minced

1 (14.5-ounce) can cannellini beans, drained and rinsed

1 (14.5-ounce) can fire-roasted diced tomatoes, juices reserved

1 (14.5-ounce) can artichoke hearts, drained, rinsed, and roughly chopped

1 teaspoon dried oregano

1 teaspoon dried thyme

2 cups roughly chopped kale

Salt and freshly ground black pepper

2 ounces feta cheese (optional)

**PER SERVING:** Calories: 229; Total fat: 5g; Carbohydrates: 41g; Fiber: 16g; Protein: 11g; Calcium: 121mg; Vitamin D: 0mcg; Vitamin B$_{12}$: 0mcg; Iron: 4mg; Zinc: 1mg

1. In a large sauté pan or skillet, heat the olive oil over medium-high heat. Sauté the onion until translucent, about 5 minutes. Add the sun-dried tomatoes and garlic, and sauté until the garlic is fragrant.

2. Add the beans, tomatoes with juices, artichokes, oregano, and thyme. Stir to combine. Reduce the heat to medium. Cover and cook for 5 to 7 minutes.

3. Uncover the skillet and stir in the kale until wilted. Season with salt and pepper to taste.

4. Serve topped with feta cheese, if using.

➤ **Prep tip:** Make sure to follow the directions indicating when to add which ingredients, because they all have different cook times. This prevents certain ingredients from becoming overcooked or undercooked.

**VARIATIONS:**

➤ **Tuscan Shrimp and White Bean Skillet:** Thaw frozen cooked shrimp and mix it in with this one-pot meal.

➤ **Roasted Red Pepper White Bean Skillet:** Swap the diced tomatoes for roasted red peppers for a slightly sweeter twist.

# Lasagna-Style Stuffed Portobello Mushrooms

SEASON:
Spring, summer, fall, winter

**VEGETARIAN**

Did you know that mushrooms are the only source of vitamin D that can be found in the produce section of the grocery store? Enjoy this quick version of lasagna to help you get your fill of the "sunshine vitamin," as well as B vitamins, selenium, and potassium.

**Serves 4 | Prep time: 10 minutes | Cook time: 30 minutes**

4 large portobello mushrooms

1 cup ricotta cheese

1 egg

2 cups finely chopped baby spinach

2 cups shredded mozzarella, divided

1 cup grated Parmesan cheese, divided

2 tablespoons chopped fresh basil, plus more for garnishing (optional)

1 teaspoon garlic powder

¼ teaspoon red pepper flakes

⅛ teaspoon ground nutmeg

½ teaspoon salt

¼ teaspoon freshly ground black pepper

1 cup Simple Marinara Sauce (page 185) or store-bought

1. Preheat the oven to 400°F. Place a rimmed rack on a sheet pan.

2. Gently scoop out the gills on the insides of the mushrooms. Discard the gills. Place the mushrooms on the wire rack, scooped-side up.

3. In a bowl, mix together the ricotta cheese, egg, spinach, 1 cup of mozzarella, ½ cup of Parmesan, the basil, garlic powder, red pepper flakes, nutmeg, salt, and black pepper.

4. Evenly divide the ricotta mixture between the mushrooms. Top each mushroom with ¼ cup marinara sauce. Top with the remaining 1 cup of mozzarella and ½ cup of Parmesan.

5. Bake the mushrooms in the oven for 25 to 30 minutes, until the cheese is melted and the mushrooms are tender. Set the oven to broil if you want the cheese to brown on top.

6. Remove from the oven and garnish with additional basil, if using.

**CONTINUED**

➤ **Prep tip:** Take the time to remove the mushroom gills. If left in, they can be bitter and create a gritty texture.

## VARIATIONS:

➤ **Lasagna-Style Stuffed Zucchini:** Cut the zucchini lengthwise. Scoop out the insides of the zucchini. Follow the same directions, but put the zucchini in the oven for 10 minutes to start to soften before stuffing with the ricotta mixture.

➤ **Stuffed Portobello Mushrooms Layered with Eggplant:** Add thinly sliced eggplant on top of the stuffed mushrooms before topping with cheese and baking.

**PER SERVING:** Calories: 455; Total fat: 30g; Carbohydrates: 16g; Fiber: 4g; Protein: 33g; Calcium: 662mg; Vitamin D: 48mcg; Vitamin $B_{12}$: 2mcg; Iron: 2mg; Zinc: 5mg

# Pesto Portobello Burgers

SEASON:
Spring, summer,
fall, winter

**VEGETARIAN**

Just thinking about this recipe makes my mouth water. These are vegetarian burgers that even a meat lover will ask for again and again. You can slice up each portobello and add it to a leafy green wrap for more veggie goodness.

**Serves 4 | Prep time: 10 minutes | Cook time: 15 minutes**

4 portobello mushrooms

2 tablespoons balsamic vinegar

2 tablespoons olive oil

Salt

Freshly ground black pepper

4 slices provolone cheese

4 burger buns

¼ cup prepared pesto

1 tomato, sliced

1 cup mixed greens

**PER SERVING:** Calories: 385; Total fat: 25g; Carbohydrates: 27g; Fiber: 2g; Protein: 15g; Calcium: 331mg; Vitamin D: 15mcg; Vitamin B$_{12}$: 1mcg; Iron: 2mg; Zinc: 2mg

1. Preheat the grill to medium-high heat.

2. Remove the stems and gills from the mushrooms. In a shallow dish, whisk together the balsamic vinegar and olive oil. Using a pastry brush, brush the mushrooms all over with the balsamic and oil mixture. Sprinkle them with salt and pepper.

3. Put the mushrooms on the grill and cook 5 minutes per side. Within the last minute of cooking, top each mushroom with the slice of provolone. Remove from the grill.

4. Place the mushrooms on burger buns and top with pesto, a slice of tomato, and mixed greens. Serve immediately.

➤ **Beyond the basics:** No grill? No problem! Make this recipe in the comfort of your home using a grill pan.

**VARIATIONS:**

➤ **Brussels Sprout Pesto Portobello Burger:** Go for veggie gold by using the Brussels Sprout Pesto (page 182) instead of a premade basil pesto.

➤ **Pesto Provolone Portobello Pizza:** You have another option to skip the bun altogether and turn this into a mini mushroom pizza by using store-bought dough or making a Cauliflower Crust Pizza (page 118).

# Roasted Brussels Sprout Tacos with Garlicky Black Bean Spread

SEASON:
Fall, winter

**VEGETARIAN**

As you might have guessed, Brussels sprouts are my favorite vegetable. Tacos are one of my favorite foods. Put them together and what do you get? A unique, flavorful taco you didn't know was missing from your life. Simple, crispy Brussels sprouts are a staple in my household, so I decided to serve them up as a filling for vegetarian tacos. Add the super-garlicky black bean spread and boy do you have a hit.

**Serves 4 to 6 | Prep time: 5 minutes | Cook time: 30 minutes**

### FOR THE TACO FILLING

1 pound Brussels sprouts, trimmed and quartered

½ white onion, chopped

1 garlic clove, minced

2 tablespoons olive oil

Salt

Freshly ground black pepper

### FOR THE BLACK BEAN SPREAD

1 (15-ounce) can black beans, drained and rinsed

1 tablespoon olive oil

1 garlic clove

Juice from 1 lime

1 tablespoon chopped fresh cilantro

1 teaspoon salt

1 teaspoon freshly ground black pepper

### FOR THE TACOS

6 corn tortillas

6 tablespoons shredded cheddar cheese

1. Preheat the oven to 400°F.

2. **To make the taco filling:** Spread the Brussels sprouts, onion, and minced garlic on a large sheet pan. Drizzle them with the olive oil and season with salt and pepper to taste. Put in the oven for 30 to 35 minutes, until the Brussels sprout leaves begin to brown.

3.  **To make the black bean spread:** While the Brussels sprouts are roasting, combine the black beans, olive oil, garlic, lime juice, cilantro, salt, and pepper in a food processor or a high-speed blender. Blend until smooth.

4.  **To make the tacos:** Set a tortilla over a burner flame for 30 to 45 seconds on each side to char.

5.  To serve, spread 1 to 2 tablespoons of the black bean mixture on a tortilla and top with the roasted Brussels sprouts mixture. Sprinkle with 1 tablespoon shredded cheddar cheese.

➤ **Make it easier:** Don't stress the spread and just use black beans to fill the tacos, adding a squeeze of lime juice and the chopped cilantro.

## VARIATIONS:

➤ **Roasted Broccoli Tacos with Garlicky Black Bean Spread:** Not a fan of sprouts? Try roasted broccoli florets instead.

➤ **Roasted Corn and Tomato Tacos with Black Bean Spread:** Swap out Brussels sprouts for roasted corn and tomatoes for a more traditional Tex-Mex taco.

**PER SERVING:** Calories: 388; Total fat: 19g; Carbohydrates: 42g; Fiber: 7g; Protein: 16g; Calcium: 269mg; Vitamin D: 5mcg; Vitamin $B_{12}$: 0mcg; Iron: 3mg; Zinc: 2mg

# Shakshuka

If you're into breakfast for dinner (and who isn't?), this one-pan meal is impressive while requiring little effort. Scale it down to make this as a single serving, or scale it up and use a larger skillet to serve a crowd.

SEASON:
Spring, summer, fall, winter

**VEGETARIAN**

**Serves 4 to 6 | Prep time: 15 minutes | Cook time: 15 minutes**

2 tablespoons olive oil

1 large onion, chopped

1 large red bell pepper, chopped

4 garlic cloves, chopped

1 teaspoon ground cumin

¾ teaspoon smoked paprika

¼ teaspoon salt

⅛ teaspoon freshly ground black pepper

¼ teaspoon red pepper flakes

2 tablespoons tomato paste

1 (28-ounce) can fire-roasted, crushed tomatoes

6 large eggs

Chopped fresh parsley

Crusty bread or pita, for serving

1. Preheat the oven to 375°F. Heat the oil in a large, oven-safe skillet (preferably cast iron) over medium-high heat. Sauté the onions and pepper; cook until the onions are translucent and tender. Add the garlic and sauté 1 minute more, or until fragrant.

2. Add the cumin, paprika, salt, black pepper, and red pepper flakes. Stir until the vegetables are coated. Stir in the tomato paste and coat the vegetables.

3. Stir in the crushed tomatoes with their juices. Reduce heat to a gentle simmer and cook for 5 minutes to let the flavors come together.

4. Turn off the heat. Make 6 small wells within the tomato mixture. Carefully crack an egg into each well.

5. Carefully transfer the skillet to the oven, and bake for 8 to 12 minutes, until the egg whites are opaque.

6. Remove the skillet from the oven and top with fresh parsley. Serve with crusty bread or pita on the side.

**PER SERVING:** Calories: 279; Total fat: 15g; Carbohydrates: 24g; Fiber: 7g; Protein: 14g; Calcium: 141mg; Vitamin D: 62mcg; Vitamin $B_{12}$: 1mcg; Iron: 4mg; Zinc: 2mg

➤ **Prep tip:** Make sure the eggs are at room temperature before adding them to the pan, because cold eggs will lower the temperature of the sauce. If you have the time, separate the egg yolks and whites, and add the whites first to cook a few minutes longer than the yolks in the wells.

**VARIATIONS:**

➤ **Green Shakshuka:** Add green bell peppers, spinach, and tomatillos to go green with this dish.

➤ **Mexican-Inspired Shakshuka:** Try a mash-up of huevos rancheros and shakshuka by adding black beans and Cotija or cheddar cheese.

# Pumpkin-Tofu Curry with Green Beans

SEASON:
Fall, winter

**VEGAN**

Curry may be intimidating for some, but this recipe uses only a few herbs and spices to create a cozy and comforting dish that will make you more courageous in the kitchen. Slightly sweet, this one-pot dish is packed with vitamin A, vitamin C, plant-based protein, and fiber.

**Serves 4 | Prep time: 5 minutes | Cook time: 25 minutes**

2 tablespoons olive oil

1 medium onion, diced

½ pound green
  beans, trimmed

2 teaspoons curry powder

2 teaspoons ground cumin

1 teaspoon ground ginger

1 (15-ounce) can coconut milk

1 cup water

1½ cups quinoa, rinsed

1 (15-ounce) can
  pumpkin puree

14 ounces extra-firm tofu,
  pressed and cubed

**PER SERVING:** Calories: 667;
Total fat: 40g; Carbohydrates: 62g;
Fiber: 11g; Protein: 24g;
Calcium: 293mg; Vitamin D: 0mcg;
Vitamin B$_{12}$: 0mcg; Iron: 11mg;
Zinc: 4mg

1. Heat the oil in a large pot, then add in the onion and cook until translucent, 10 to 15 minutes.

2. Add in the green beans, curry powder, cumin, ginger, coconut milk, water, and quinoa, stirring to combine. Bring to a boil and then reduce the heat to simmer for 15 minutes.

3. Mix in the pumpkin puree and tofu cubes, continuing to cook 5 to 7 minutes more.

➤ **Make it easier:** Look for a premade curry spice blend that can be used with a lot of different vegetable dishes.

**VARIATIONS:**

➤ **Spicy Sweet Potato Curry with Green Beans:** Replace the pumpkin puree with mashed sweet potato and heat things up with 1 diced jalapeño or red pepper flakes.

➤ **Butternut Squash and Brown Rice Curry with Tofu:** Use brown rice in place of quinoa, and cubed butternut squash instead of pumpkin puree.

# Lentil Bolognese over Spaghetti

SEASON:
Spring, summer, fall, winter

**VEGETARIAN, VEGAN OPTION** (see headnote)

Talk about a meal that gives you the most bang for your buck! This lentil Bolognese will win over even the biggest carnivore in your life. Try it with regular or whole-wheat pasta, but if you want something lighter, serve this over zucchini noodles. And you can easily turn this vegan by skipping the yogurt.

**Serves 4 | Prep time: 15 minutes | Cook time: 50 minutes**

2 tablespoons olive oil

2 carrots, peeled and diced

1 onion, diced

1 celery stalk, diced

½ teaspoon salt

1 cup green lentils, rinsed

1 (14.5-ounce) can diced tomatoes, with juices

4 cups vegetable broth

⅛ teaspoon freshly ground black pepper

2 tablespoons plain Greek yogurt

1 tablespoon balsamic vinegar

1 pound whole-wheat spaghetti

1. Heat a pot over medium heat, then pour in the oil. Add the carrots, onion, celery, and salt, and sauté until translucent or slightly golden, 8 to 10 minutes.

2. Add the lentils, tomatoes, and broth, and bring to a boil. Lower the heat and let it simmer until the lentils are cooked through, 25 to 30 minutes. Stir in the pepper, yogurt, and vinegar, and continue to simmer.

3. As the Bolognese is cooking, prepare the spaghetti according to the package directions.

4. Divide the spaghetti into 4 bowls and spoon the lentil Bolognese on top.

➤ **Prep tip:** Use green or brown lentils for sauces and stews, as they hold their shape better than red or yellow ones.

**PER SERVING:** Calories: 684; Total fat: 9g; Carbohydrates: 128g; Fiber: 18g; Protein: 30g; Calcium: 125mg; Vitamin D: 0mcg; Vitamin B$_{12}$: 0mcg; Iron: 8mg; Zinc: 5mg

### VARIATIONS:

➤ **Lentil Mushroom Bolognese:** Add 1 to 2 cups of chopped mushrooms when simmering the sauce.

➤ **Beef and Beet Bolognese:** Swap the lentils for 1 pound cooked ground beef and add 1 roasted and shredded beet into the sauce.

# Sloppy Joe–Stuffed Peppers

SEASON:
Spring, summer,
fall, winter

VEGAN

These stuffed peppers have all the flavor of a traditional sloppy joe with way more plant power and a lot less mess. If you are more of a meat-a-tarian, feel free to mix in some ground beef with the lentils to bulk things up. Serve these as they are or with a toasted brioche bun on the side.

**Serves 4 | Prep time: 5 minutes | Cook time: 60 minutes**

1 cup green lentils

2 cups vegetable broth

4 bell peppers, any color

2 tablespoons olive oil

½ cup sliced mushrooms

½ cup diced carrots

1 onion, chopped

1 (14.5-ounce) can crushed tomatoes

1 tablespoon balsamic vinegar

1 tablespoon soy sauce

1 teaspoon brown sugar

**PER SERVING:** Calories: 352; Total fat: 8g; Carbohydrates: 59g; Fiber: 10g; Protein: 16g; Calcium: 70mg; Vitamin D: 1mcg; Vitamin $B_{12}$: 0mcg; Iron: 6mg; Zinc: 2mg

1. In a medium pot, bring the lentils and the broth to a boil. Once boiling, reduce the heat and simmer until the broth has been absorbed and the lentils are tender, about 25 minutes. Set aside.

2. Preheat the oven to 375°F.

3. Prepare the bell peppers by slicing them in half and removing the seeds and ribs. Arrange the peppers in a casserole dish or on a sheet pan, the open side facing up.

4. Heat the olive oil in a medium saucepan. Add the mushrooms and sauté until brown. Stir in the carrots and cook for 5 minutes. Add the onion and stir, cooking for 2 to 3 minutes more.

5. Stir the tomatoes, vinegar, soy sauce, and brown sugar into the mushroom mixture. Simmer for about 10 minutes.

6. Stir the cooked lentils into the mushroom mixture until well combined.

7. Fill the pepper halves with the lentil mixture, put them in the oven, and bake for 35 minutes. If you prefer softer peppers, bake 5 to 10 minutes more.

**CONTINUED**

# Sloppy Joe–Stuffed Peppers CONTINUED

➤ **Prep tip:** Save time by cooking a big batch of lentils in advance or purchasing them precooked.

## VARIATIONS:

➤ **Sloppy Joe–Stuffed Tomatoes:** Following the above directions, fill large, scooped-out tomatoes and bake them for 15 minutes, or until the tomatoes soften slightly.

➤ **Vegan Sloppy Joe Soup:** Dice the peppers and stir all ingredients into a pot with a large can of condensed tomato soup.

# Shepherd's Pie–Stuffed Sweet Potatoes

SEASON:
Fall, winter

**VEGAN**

This is not your mama's twice-baked potato! Just a few ingredients come together nicely for this hearty vegan twist on shepherd's pie. The plant-powered protein from lentils combines with fiber, vitamins, and minerals in the veggies for a filling and nutritious dish you can prepare ahead of time.

**Serves 4 | Prep time: 5 minutes | Cook time: 70 minutes**

4 medium sweet potatoes

2 tablespoons olive oil

2 medium carrots, diced

2 celery stalks, diced

½ large onion, diced

1 cup cooked lentils

1 (15-ounce) can
    diced tomatoes

---

**PER SERVING:** Calories: 267;
Total fat: 7g; Carbohydrates: 45g;
Fiber: 11g; Protein: 8g;
Calcium: 101mg; Vitamin D: 0mcg;
Vitamin B$_{12}$: 0mcg; Iron: 3mg;
Zinc: 1mg

1. Preheat the oven to 400°F. Scrub the sweet potatoes and puncture them with a fork. Put them on a sheet pan and bake for 50 minutes.

2. While potatoes are baking, heat the olive oil in a sauté pan over medium heat. Add in the diced carrots, celery, and onion, cover, and cook about 10 minutes. Add the cooked lentils and diced tomatoes, and stir until well combined. Set aside.

3. Remove the potatoes from the oven and let them cool for a few minutes. Slice off the top third of the potato lengthwise and scoop the insides of the potatoes into a food processor or blender. Pulse until the potatoes are whipped (adding a little water if necessary).

4. Fill the sweet potato shells with approximately ⅓ cup of the lentil mixture. Top each potato with the mashed sweet potatoes and return them to the oven to bake for 20 minutes more.

**CONTINUED**

➤ **Beyond the basics:** Make these spuds look fancy by using a pastry bag or by spooning the potato mixture into a large resealable bag, and cutting the corner to pipe it on top.

## VARIATIONS:

➤ **Traditional Shepherd's Pie-Stuffed Potatoes:** Using sweet potatoes or large russet potatoes, replace the lentils with cooked ground beef or lamb for a more traditional take on shepherd's pie.

➤ **Spicy Stuffed Sweet Potatoes:** Omit the carrots and celery, and add in corn, black beans, and green bell peppers, along with paprika and chili powder.

# Sweet Potato Burgers

These sweet potato burgers check off so many boxes in terms of flavor and nutrition. They're so much better than any store-bought veggie burger patty you've ever tried and probably cheaper, too. Serve this with a simple side dish like the Broccoli-Pear Slaw (page 67).

**SEASON:**
Spring, summer, fall, winter

**VEGETARIAN**

**Serves 6 | Prep time: 15 minutes | Cook time: 30 minutes**

1 large sweet potato
1 (15-ounce) can cannellini
  beans, drained and rinsed
¼ cup small dice red onion
½ cup panko bread crumbs
1 teaspoon cumin
1 teaspoon smoked paprika
½ teaspoon garlic powder
½ teaspoon salt
½ cup mayonnaise
1 tablespoon sriracha
6 burger buns

**PER SERVING:** Calories: 352; Total fat: 16g; Carbohydrates: 42g; Fiber: 7g; Protein: 11g; Calcium: 131mg; Vitamin D: 1mcg; Vitamin B$_{12}$: 0mcg; Iron: 4mg; Zinc: 1mg

1. Preheat the oven to 400°F. Coat a sheet pan with cooking spray. Set aside for later use.

2. Gently wrap the sweet potato in aluminum foil. Bake in the oven for 40 to 50 minutes, until the sweet potato is fork-tender.

3. Let the sweet potato cool until it can be handled. Scrape the flesh from the skin and put it in a large bowl. Add the beans and mash using a potato masher, leaving some beans intact.

4. Mix in the onion, bread crumbs, cumin, paprika, garlic powder, and salt until well combined.

5. Scoop ½ cup of the burger mixture and form a burger shape. Repeat, forming 6 burgers. Place them on the sheet pan. Bake them for 30 minutes, flipping halfway through cooking.

6. In a small bowl, mix together the mayonnaise and sriracha.

7. Serve the burgers on buns and top with sriracha mayo and additional toppings, such as lettuce, tomato, onion, and avocado, if desired.

**CONTINUED**

## Sweet Potato Burgers  CONTINUED

> **Prep tip:** Make the burger mixture ahead of time by form-
> ing it into patties and individually freezing each for use later.

### VARIATIONS:

> **Sweet Potato–Mushroom Burgers:** Add 1 finely
> chopped portobello mushroom to the sweet potato mixture
> for a heartier texture.

> **Beet and Black Bean Burgers:** Use 1 shredded beet in
> place of the sweet potato and swap the cannellini beans for
> black beans.

# Sweet Potato Sheet Pan Nachos

SEASON:
Spring, summer, fall, winter

**VEGETARIAN**

This recipe has quickly become a go-to on our weekly dinner meal plan, especially because it's easy to make swaps and substitutions for whatever veggies and toppings you happen to have on hand. Serve this as an appetizer at your next gathering or for a fun, nontraditional dinner option.

**Serves 4 | Prep time: 10 minutes | Cook time: 50 minutes**

2 sweet potatoes, peeled and cut into ¼-inch rounds

1 tablespoon olive oil

1 teaspoon garlic powder

½ teaspoon ground cumin

¼ teaspoon salt

⅛ teaspoon freshly ground black pepper

1 (14.5-ounce) can corn, drained and rinsed

1 (14.5-ounce) can black beans, drained and rinsed

½ cup halved grape tomatoes

½ cup pickled jalapeño pepper slices

1 cup shredded cheddar cheese

½ cup salsa

Avocado, for topping (optional)

Greek yogurt or sour cream, for topping (optional)

1. Preheat the oven to 425°F. Coat a sheet pan with cooking spray.

2. Toss the sweet potatoes with the olive oil, garlic powder, cumin, salt, and black pepper. Arrange the sweet potatoes in an even layer on the sheet pan. Roast for 40 minutes, until fork-tender, flipping halfway through.

3. When the sweet potatoes are done, arrange them on the sheet pan piled up on one another, nacho-style. Spread the corn, beans, tomatoes, jalapeños, and cheese evenly on top.

4. Bake 5 to 7 minutes more.

5. Top with salsa and other toppings, as desired.

➤ **Make it easier:** Use a mandoline for very thin sweet potato slices that will be more like traditional tortilla chips.

**CONTINUED**

## Sweet Potato Sheet Pan Nachos <small>CONTINUED</small>

**VARIATIONS:**

➤ **Irish Pub Nachos:** Use white potatoes and skip the corn and black beans for a more traditional barroom dish.

➤ **Veggie-Loaded Sweet Potato Fries:** Play with texture by cutting potatoes into thick wedges instead of slices.

**PER SERVING:** Calories: 375; Total fat: 15g; Carbohydrates: 48g; Fiber: 11g; Protein: 16g; Calcium: 246mg; Vitamin D: 7mcg; Vitamin $B_{12}$: 0mcg; Iron: 3mg; Zinc: 2mg

# Ricotta-Spinach Calzones

SEASON:
Spring, summer, fall, winter

VEGETARIAN

I like to think of calzones as folded-up pizza tacos, and these are filled with one of my favorite leafy greens. Don't skip the egg wash—it'll give the calzones a shiny, crusty outside that you'll be excited to dig into with your knife and fork.

**Makes 4 servings | Prep time: 15 minutes | Cook time: 15 minutes**

2 cups finely chopped spinach

8 ounces ricotta cheese

4 ounces mozzarella, shredded

1 tablespoon olive oil

1 large egg yolk

1 teaspoon garlic powder

2 teaspoons dried oregano

⅛ teaspoon red pepper flakes

1 teaspoon salt

1 pound pizza dough

1 large egg, lightly beaten with
   2 tablespoons water

1 ounce grated
   Parmesan cheese

2 cups Simple Marinara Sauce
   (page 185) or store-bought

**PER SERVING:** Calories: 587;
Total fat: 25g; Carbohydrates: 64g;
Fiber: 5g; Protein: 28g;
Calcium: 396mg; Vitamin D: 31mcg;
Vitamin B$_{12}$: 1mcg; Iron: 5mg;
Zinc: 2mg

1. Preheat the oven to 500°F. Line a sheet pan with parchment paper.

2. Combine the spinach, ricotta, mozzarella, olive oil, egg yolk, garlic powder, oregano, red pepper flakes, and salt in a large bowl.

3. Place the dough on a lightly floured surface and divide it into 4 pieces. With a rolling pin, flatten each piece into a 7-inch round.

4. Spread one-quarter of the spinach filling evenly over half of each dough round, leaving a 1-inch border around the edge.

5. Brush the edges with the egg wash and then fold the other half of the dough circle over the spinach mixture, leaving the bottom ½-inch border uncovered.

6. Press the edges of the dough together and pinch them with your fingers to seal.

7. With a sharp knife, cut 3 steam vents in the top of the calzones, and brush the tops with the egg wash.

**CONTINUED**

## Ricotta-Spinach Calzones CONTINUED

8. Transfer the calzones to the sheet pan and bake for 8 minutes, brush with any remaining egg wash and sprinkle with grated Parmesan, and then bake for another 7 minutes.

9. Move the calzones to a wire rack and let cool for 5 minutes before serving. Serve with the marinara sauce.

➤ **Prep tip:** Using frozen pizza dough? Let it rest and come to room temperature for at least 30 minutes before rolling out.

### VARIATIONS:

➤ **Breakfast Spinach-Feta Calzones:** Scramble the eggs, spinach, and feta, then wrap in pizza dough and bake.
➤ **Broccoli Calzones:** Replace well-chopped broccoli for spinach and add a squeeze of lemon juice to the calzone filling.

# Spinach and Artichoke Mac and Cheese

SEASON:
Fall, winter

VEGETARIAN

This one shouldn't take much convincing to try. If you're a fan of mac and cheese and/or spinach artichoke dip, this is your gateway vegetable recipe. It's a comfort food casserole that works well on a cool fall or winter night.

**Serves 4 | Prep time: 15 minutes | Cook time: 55 minutes**

1 pound conchiglie (shell) pasta, cooked

3 tablespoons butter

2 tablespoons all-purpose flour

3 cups milk

1 teaspoon salt

½ teaspoon freshly ground black pepper

8 ounces sharp cheddar cheese, shredded, divided

9 ounces frozen spinach, thawed and drained well

2 (14-ounce) cans artichoke hearts, drained and chopped

1 cup panko bread crumbs

**PER SERVING:** Calories: 774; Total fat: 37g; Carbohydrates: 80g; Fiber: 19g; Protein: 35g; Calcium: 744mg; Vitamin D: 24mcg; Vitamin $B_{12}$: 1mcg; Iron: 4mg; Zinc: 4mg

1. Preheat the oven to 350°F. Spray a 9-by-13-inch baking dish with cooking spray. Cook the pasta according to the package directions.

2. In a large saucepan, create a roux by melting the butter until gently bubbling. Whisk in the flour until it's absorbed and turns a light amber color.

3. Whisk in the milk, salt, and pepper. Keep whisking until thickened.

4. Using a wooden spoon, stir in three-quarters of the cheese and the spinach and artichokes. Reduce the mixture to a low simmer, continuing to stir.

5. Add the pasta to the cheese mixture and stir well. Once incorporated, transfer to the baking dish. Top with the remaining cheese and the bread crumbs.

6. Bake for 45 minutes, or until the cheese is bubbling and the top is browned.

**CONTINUED**

# Spinach and Artichoke Mac and Cheese CONTINUED

➤ **Prep tip:** As the cheese is melting, stir constantly so it doesn't scorch the bottom of the pot.

## VARIATIONS:

➤ **Butternut Squash Mac and Cheese:** Instead of spinach and artichokes, stir 1½ pounds of cooked and pureed butternut squash in with the pasta and cheese. Bake as directed.

➤ **Kale Artichoke Mac and Cheese:** Sub in well-chopped kale for spinach leaves.

# Tortellini with Mushrooms and Sage

VEGETARIAN

This quick and easy meal takes traditional tortellini up a notch with cremini mushrooms and sage, a flavor combo that's fail-proof. Serve this any time of year for a cozy, satisfying meal. It even works with frozen tortellini or ravioli.

**Serves 4 | Prep time: 15 minutes | Cook time: 20 minutes**

1 (25-ounce) package
   refrigerated fresh
   cheese tortellini
2 tablespoons butter
1 tablespoon olive oil
8 ounces cremini
   mushrooms, sliced
2 garlic cloves, minced
2 tablespoons chopped
   fresh sage
½ cup grated Parmesan cheese
Salt
Freshly ground black pepper

1. Bring a large pot of water to a boil. Add a pinch of salt and cook the tortellini according to package directions.

2. In a large sauté pan or skillet over medium-high heat, combine the butter and olive oil. Once the butter melts and begins to gently bubble, add the mushrooms. Sauté for 5 to 7 minutes, until the mushrooms have softened and browned. Add the garlic and cook for 1 more minute, or until fragrant. Add the sage and Parmesan and toss to mix all ingredients.

3. Add the drained tortellini to the pan and toss to combine. Season with salt and pepper to taste. Serve immediately.

**PER SERVING:** Calories: 694; Total fat: 26g; Carbohydrates: 88g; Fiber: 4g; Protein: 29g; Calcium: 390mg; Vitamin D: 11mcg; Vitamin B$_{12}$: 0mcg; Iron: 3mg; Zinc: 3mg

➤ **Prep tip:** Resist the urge to stir the mushrooms around when they cook. Letting them brown and caramelize brings out the best flavor.

**VARIATIONS:**

➤ **Tortellini with Mushroom Bolognese:** Stir the chopped mushrooms into a 15-ounce jar of tomato sauce to serve over tortellini.

➤ **Broccoli Sage Tortellini:** Simply replace the mushrooms with chopped broccoli florets for a crunchy twist.

Greek Grilled Chicken Bowl, 165

# CHAPTER 7

# Seafood and Meat Mains

# Shrimp en Papillote with Lemon Zucchini

**SEASON:** Summer

*En papillote* refers to a moist-heat cooking method where the food is enclosed in a packet of parchment paper or foil and then cooked in the oven. It may sound fancy, but it's a fast and easy dinner that's worth turning on the oven for, even in the summer.

**Serves 4 | Prep time: 10 minutes | Cook time: 25 minutes**

2 tablespoons olive oil

1 teaspoon dried rosemary

½ teaspoon salt

¼ teaspoon freshly ground black pepper

2 zucchini, cut into quarters

2 garlic cloves, minced

1 pound raw shrimp, shelled and deveined

½ lemon, sliced thin

Chopped parsley, for garnish (optional)

**PER SERVING:** Calories: 161; Total fat: 8g; Carbohydrates: 5g; Fiber: 1g; Protein: 17g; Calcium: 84mg; Vitamin D: 2mcg; Vitamin B$_{12}$: 1mcg; Iron: 1mg; Zinc: 1mg

1. Preheat the oven to 425°F.

2. In a small bowl, mix the oil, rosemary, salt, and pepper.

3. Cut 4 (10-by-10-inch) squares of parchment paper and fold each in half.

4. Open the parchment paper and place a quarter of the zucchini and garlic in the middle of one side. Place one-quarter of the shrimp on top. Drizzle with some of the olive oil mixture. Place a few lemon slices on top.

5. Fold the edges to create a pouch, leaving some air within the pouch. Repeat with the remaining pieces of parchment paper and ingredients.

6. Place the pouches on a sheet pan. Bake for 20 to 25 minutes.

7. Open the pouches and sprinkle with parsley, if using.

➤ **Beyond the basics:** Make these on an outdoor grill by using foil instead of parchment.

**CONTINUED**

**VARIATIONS:**

➤ **Cod en Papillote:** Swap out the shrimp for cod. Mix and match quick-cooking vegetables like asparagus or sugar snap peas.

➤ **Lemon, Asparagus, and Shrimp en Papillote:** Asparagus is a great sub for zucchini in this recipe, pairing well with both shrimp and lemon.

# Shrimp Stir-Fry with Bok Choy and Broccoli

SEASON:
Fall, winter

Serve this simple stir-fry over brown rice or quinoa, or with noodles to soak up the sauce. Or enjoy all by itself. The vitamins and minerals in the bok choy and broccoli combine with the protein in the shrimp for a nutritious meal that satisfies.

**Serves 4 to 6 | Prep time: 5 minutes | Cook time: 10 minutes**

2 tablespoons olive oil

2 garlic cloves, minced

1 pound shrimp, peeled and deveined

1 pound baby bok choy (about 6 bunches), trimmed and sliced in half

1 cup broccoli florets

½ cup vegetable broth

¼ cup low-sodium soy sauce

2 tablespoons apple cider vinegar

½ teaspoon garlic powder

¼ teaspoon ground ginger

**PER SERVING:** Calories: 179; Total fat: 8g; Carbohydrates: 7g; Fiber: 2g; Protein: 19g; Calcium: 200mg; Vitamin D: 2mcg; Vitamin $B_{12}$: 1mcg; Iron: 2mg; Zinc: 2mg

1. In a large sauté pan or skillet, heat the oil and garlic. Add in the shrimp and cook for 2 to 3 minutes.

2. Next, add the bok choy and broccoli florets to the pan, cooking 2 to 3 more minutes, or until the bok choy begins to brown. Add the vegetable broth to the pan and lower the heat to simmer.

3. In a small bowl, combine the soy sauce, vinegar, garlic powder, and ginger.

4. Add the soy sauce mixture to the pan and serve immediately.

➤ **Prep tip:** For smaller pieces, stack the bok choy leaves and slice into small strips.

**VARIATIONS:**

➤ **Mushroom, Bok Choy, and Shrimp Stir-Fry:** Replace the broccoli with 1 to 2 cups sliced mushrooms.

➤ **Broccoli and Pea Shrimp Stir-Fry:** Swap in 2 cups of green peas for the bok choy.

# Quick Shrimp Pad Thai

SEASON:
Spring, summer,
fall, winter

Commonly served by street vendors in Thailand, pad Thai combines veggies, rice noodles, eggs, protein, and nuts. This veggie-loaded version has big flavor and will be a welcome addition to your recipe repertoire in no time.

**Serves 6 | Prep time: 10 minutes | Cook time: 15 minutes**

1 (10-ounce) package Thai rice noodles

2 tablespoons brown sugar

¼ cup low-sodium soy sauce

1 tablespoon lime juice

1 tablespoon fish sauce

1 tablespoon canola oil

1 large red bell pepper, thinly sliced

1 cup shredded carrots

2 garlic cloves, minced

4 scallions, both white and green parts, thinly sliced

3 eggs, beaten

1 pound cooked, peeled, deveined frozen shrimp, thawed

½ cup chopped unsalted peanuts

⅓ cup chopped cilantro

---

**PER SERVING:** Calories: 393; Total fat: 12g; Carbohydrates: 50g; Fiber: 3g; Protein: 21g; Calcium: 95mg; Vitamin D: 22mcg; Vitamin $B_{12}$: 1mcg; Iron: 2mg; Zinc: 2mg

1. Cook the rice noodles according to the package directions.

2. In a small bowl, combine the brown sugar, soy sauce, lime juice, and fish sauce. Set aside.

3. In a large sauté pan or skillet, heat the oil over medium-high heat. Add the pepper and carrots, and cook for 2 minutes. Add the garlic and scallions, then continue to sauté until fragrant.

4. Push the vegetables to the edges of the pan, creating a well in the center. Pour in the eggs and gently stir to create scrambled eggs. Add the shrimp, noodles, and sauce, and mix well to combine until heated through.

5. Remove from heat and top with peanuts and cilantro.

➤ **Beyond the basics:** If you have access to a wok, use it. Woks are designed to heat quickly and allow for the efficient movement of all the ingredients.

---

## VARIATIONS:

➤ **Chicken Pad Thai:** Cook the chicken in the pan before sautéing the vegetables. Remove the chicken from the pan and add it back in when adding the noodles.

➤ **Shrimp Pad Thai with Snow Peas:** Replace the carrots or bell pepper with snow peas for a similar crunch.

# Tuna Collard Wraps

SEASON:
Winter, spring

The first time I tried a collard wrap, I was skeptical, thinking it could never work as a suitable replacement for the tried-and-true tortilla. And I was right . . . but while the collards may not *replace* tortillas in your diet, it's still an amazing alternative, especially if you're looking to switch things up and enjoy more veggies.

**Serves 4 | Prep time: 15 minutes | Cook time: 3 minutes**

4 large collard greens leaves, stems removed

2 (5-ounce) cans tuna, drained

2 medium celery stalks, diced

3 tablespoons mayonnaise

Juice from 1 lemon

½ cup shredded carrots

1 avocado, sliced

---

**PER SERVING:** Calories: 231; Total fat: 16g; Carbohydrates: 10g; Fiber: 6g; Protein: 14g; Calcium: 110mg; Vitamin D: 27mcg; Vitamin B$_{12}$: 1mcg; Iron: 1mg; Zinc: 1mg

1. Bring a shallow pan of water to a gentle simmer. Blanch the collard greens in boiling water for 30 seconds, then place them in a bowl filled with ice and water. This will help the greens become more pliable.

2. In a small bowl, mix together the tuna (breaking up the large chunks), celery, mayonnaise, and lemon juice.

3. Pat dry a collard leaf, add a quarter of the tuna mixture, and top with some carrots and avocado.

4. Wrap up like you would a burrito. Repeat with the rest of the ingredients.

➤ **Prep tip:** If the stalk of the collard greens is still pretty thick after removing the excess stem, slide your knife gently down to make the leaf more pliable for wrapping.

---

**VARIATIONS:**

➤ **Rainbow Chard Tuna Wraps:** Swap out the collard greens for bright and beautiful rainbow chard leaves.

➤ **Tuna Collard Wraps with Cucumber Sticks:** Julienne half a cucumber to use in place of celery for this recipe.

# Salmon Cakes over Sesame-Ginger Slaw

SEASON:
Spring, summer, fall, winter

There's nothing wrong with grilled salmon and vegetables, but I have faith that you can put your new veggie knowledge and culinary skills to work with these salmon cakes served over a sweet and spicy veggie slaw.

**Serves 4 | Prep time: 15 minutes | Cook time: 30 minutes**

---

### FOR THE SALMON CAKES

1 (15-ounce) can salmon, drained
1 egg, beaten
½ cup panko bread crumbs
¼ cup sour cream
2 teaspoons Dijon mustard
1 teaspoon horseradish sauce
1 teaspoon lemon juice
1 teaspoon garlic powder
2 tablespoons finely chopped fresh parsley

### FOR THE SLAW

2 cups finely shredded red cabbage
2 cups finely shredded green cabbage
1 cup shredded carrots
3 scallions, thinly sliced
1 tablespoon sesame seeds

### FOR THE DRESSING

¼ cup rice vinegar
½ tablespoon honey
1 tablespoon soy sauce
½ tablespoon grated fresh ginger
Salt
Freshly ground black pepper

1. **To make the salmon cakes:** In a large bowl, mix together the salmon, egg, bread crumbs, sour cream, Dijon mustard, horseradish sauce, lemon juice, and garlic powder, breaking apart the bigger chunks of salmon. Gently stir in the parsley. Create 4 patties about ½ inch thick. Heat a sauté pan or skillet over medium-high heat. Generously coat the skillet with cooking spray. Brown the salmon cakes on both sides until golden brown.

2. **To make the slaw and dressing:** In a large bowl, combine the cabbages, carrots, scallions, and sesame seeds. In a mason jar, combine the rice vinegar, honey, soy sauce, and ginger. Secure the lid and shake to combine. Season with salt and pepper to taste. Dress slaw and toss to combine.

3. Serve each salmon cake on top of sesame-ginger slaw.

➤ **Prep tip:** Use a fish spatula, which is more flexible than a regular spatula, to flip the salmon cake with ease.

## VARIATIONS:

➤ **Salmon Cakes with Bok Choy Slaw:** No cabbage? No problem. Swap in thinly sliced bok choy instead.

➤ **Salmon Cakes with Broccoli-Pear Slaw:** Serve the salmon cakes over the Broccoli-Pear Slaw (page 67).

**PER SERVING:** Calories: 279; Total fat: 11g; Carbohydrates: 19g; Fiber: 4g; Protein: 28g; Calcium: 131mg; Vitamin D: 743mcg; Vitamin $B_{12}$: 5mcg; Iron: 2mg; Zinc: 1mg

# One-Pan Lemony Leek Risotto with Salmon

SEASON:
Spring

**VEGETARIAN OPTION**
(see Variations)

Leeks and lemon add a bright but mild flavor to this simple risotto with salmon. Wine adds a little acidity to balance things out, but it's okay to skip it altogether, or to just sip it on the side while cooking.

**Serves 4 | Prep time: 5 minutes | Cook time: 40 minutes**

2 tablespoons olive oil

2 garlic cloves, minced

½ medium onion, diced

2 leeks, sliced, light-green parts only

1 cup arborio rice

½ cup white wine (optional)

2 tablespoons lemon juice

4 cups vegetable broth

12 ounces cooked salmon (fresh or canned)

½ lemon, thinly sliced, for garnishing

**PER SERVING:** Calories: 380; Total fat: 11g; Carbohydrates: 50g; Fiber: 2g; Protein: 21g; Calcium: 239mg; Vitamin D: 411mcg; Vitamin B$_{12}$: 4mcg; Iron: 2mg; Zinc: 1mg

1. Heat the oil in a large sauté pan or skillet over medium heat, then add in the garlic, onion, and leeks, and cook for 2 to 3 minutes, until aromatic.

2. Add the rice until it begins to toast, then stir in the wine, if using, and the lemon juice. Let the rice soak up the liquid before adding the broth.

3. Turn up the heat and add the broth slowly, continuously stirring as you pour. Just before the broth begins to boil, lower the temperature and let the rice cook for 15 to 20 minutes, or until all the liquid is absorbed.

4. Stir in the salmon and portion out. Garnish with lemon slices.

➤ **Prep tip:** Don't skip toasting the rice before adding in your liquids, because this helps prevent the rice from absorbing liquid too quickly and becoming mushy.

**VARIATIONS:**

➤ **Mushroom and Pea Risotto:** Skip the salmon altogether and add mushrooms and peas for a vegetarian meal with unique texture and taste.

➤ **Asparagus Risotto with Salmon:** Swap the leeks for asparagus chopped into 2-inch pieces.

# Chicken Fried Rice

Veggies? Check. Protein? Check. Big flavor on a small budget? Check and check. This homemade version of Chinese takeout is perfect for when a craving strikes, as you likely have most of the ingredients ready to go.

SEASON:
Spring, summer, fall, winter

**VEGETARIAN OPTION**
(see Variations)

**Serves 4 | Prep time: 15 minutes | Cook time: 25 minutes**

3 tablespoons canola oil, divided

2 cups cooked white rice

6 ounces boneless, skinless chicken breast, diced

1 onion, diced

1 medium carrot, diced

3 scallions, green parts only, thinly sliced

2 garlic cloves, minced

1 cup frozen green peas

1 tablespoon low-sodium soy sauce

2 teaspoons toasted sesame oil

1 tablespoon rice wine vinegar

2 eggs, lightly beaten

Salt

Freshly ground black pepper

**PER SERVING:** Calories: 367; Total fat: 16g; Carbohydrates: 37g; Fiber: 3g; Protein: 17g; Calcium: 45mg; Vitamin D: 18mcg; Vitamin B$_{12}$: 0mcg; Iron: 3mg; Zinc: 1mg

1. In a large sauté pan or skillet, heat 1 tablespoon of oil over high heat. Add the rice and cook for 3 to 4 minutes, stirring constantly, until the rice begins to toast. Transfer to a small bowl and set aside.

2. Turn down the heat to medium and heat 1 tablespoon of oil. Add the chicken and cook for 3 to 5 minutes, until the internal temperature reaches 165°F and it begins to brown. Transfer to a plate and set aside.

3. Heat the remaining 1 tablespoon of oil and add the onion and carrot. Cook until the onion and carrot are tender. Add the scallions and garlic and cook for 1 more minute, or until fragrant. Add the peas, rice, and chicken and stir to combine.

4. Add the soy sauce, sesame oil, and rice wine vinegar. Stir to combine.

5. Make a well in the center of the skillet. Add the eggs and gently stir them to scramble. Once scrambled, break up the eggs and mix them well with the rest of the ingredients.

6. Season with salt and pepper to taste.

**CONTINUED**

# Chicken Fried Rice CONTINUED

 **Prep tip:** Be sure to use a large skillet or sauté pan to allow everything to cook quickly and evenly, and so you can toss and stir ingredients without losing any.

## VARIATIONS:

> **Vegetarian Fried Rice:** Skip the chicken and mix in edamame, beans, or tempeh.

> **Broccoli Chicken Fried Rice:** Use well-chopped broccoli in place of peas.

# Greek Grilled Chicken Bowl

Greece is still a dream travel destination for me, but I try to enjoy Greek flavors as often as I can. This bowl brings together Mediterranean veggies, lean protein, and powerful flavor from the lemon and feta. This is the perfect reason to get the grill out for a simple summer meal. But if you don't have one, these are also easily made on the stove top with a grill pan.

**Serves 4 | Prep time: 10 minutes | Cook time: 15 minutes**

4 boneless skinless
  chicken breasts

1 pound asparagus, trimmed

½ teaspoon salt

⅛ teaspoon freshly ground
  black pepper

2 cups cooked quinoa

1 (8-ounce) jar
  artichoke hearts

1 cucumber, sliced

8 ounces crumbled feta cheese

1 (10-ounce) jar pitted
  kalamata olives

1 (15-ounce) can chickpeas,
  drained and rinsed

1 lemon, sliced into wedges

1. Preheat the grill or a stove-top griddle. Season the chicken and asparagus spears with salt and pepper, then place on the grill and cook for 5 to 7 minutes. Flip and cook for 5 to 7 minutes more, or until the chicken reaches an internal temperature of 165°F. Remove from the grill and let rest.

2. To serve, put ¼ cup of quinoa into each of the four bowls, top with 2 ounces artichoke hearts, some cucumber slices, 2 ounces feta cheese, 2½ ounces olives, and about 4 ounces chickpeas.

3. Slice the grilled chicken breasts and mix them in the bowl with several asparagus spears. Serve with a lemon wedge.

➤ **Make it easier:** For a truly no-cook meal, buy a rotisserie chicken to serve on top of this bowl.

**CONTINUED**

# Greek Grilled Chicken Bowl

**VARIATIONS:**

➤ **Tex-Mex Chicken Bowl:** Use black beans, corn, roasted red peppers, and shredded cheddar in place of the artichokes, cucumbers, olives, chickpeas, and feta.

➤ **Sheet Pan Greek Chicken:** Spread the seasoned chicken and asparagus on one large sheet pan and cook in an oven at 350°F for 10 to 12 minutes. Put the artichokes, olives, and chickpeas on a second sheet pan and roast them in the same oven for about 5 minutes. Serve warm, topped with feta.

**PER SERVING:** Calories: 598; Total fat: 24g; Carbohydrates: 52g; Fiber: 14g; Protein: 47g; Calcium: 442mg; Vitamin D: 10mcg; Vitamin B$_{12}$: 1mcg; Iron: 8mg; Zinc: 5mg

# Pesto Chicken and Smashed Potatoes

**SEASON:**
Spring, summer, fall, winter

A recipe that feeds four people, uses just three ingredients, and leaves you with only two pans to clean up after cooking? Yes, please. Feel free to add even more veggies to this dish or enjoy the herb-filled potato goodness alone.

**Serves 4 | Prep time: 20 minutes | Cook time: 60 minutes**

---

1 pound mini potatoes

4 boneless skinless chicken breasts

Salt and freshly ground black pepper

1½ cups Broccoli-Basil Pesto (page 182) or store-bought

---

**PER SERVING:** Calories: 720; Total fat: 54g; Carbohydrates: 24g; Fiber: 3g; Protein: 37g; Calcium: 239mg; Vitamin D: 5mcg; Vitamin $B_{12}$: 1mcg; Iron: 3mg; Zinc: 3mg

1. Fill a large pot with water and add the potatoes. Bring the water to a boil and cook the potatoes until they are fork-tender, about 20 minutes. Drain and let cool.

2. Preheat the oven to 400°F. Line a sheet pan with parchment paper.

3. Sprinkle the chicken with salt and pepper. Arrange the chicken and potatoes on the sheet pan.

4. Using the back of a fork, gently smash the potatoes. With a pastry brush, generously brush the chicken and potatoes with pesto.

5. Cook for 40 minutes, or until the chicken is cooked to an internal temperature of 165°F, and the potatoes are crispy.

➤ **Prep tip:** Look for microwaveable mini potatoes in a bag, so you can save time and skip step 1.

---

**VARIATIONS:**

➤ **Pesto Broccoli Chicken:** Add fresh or frozen broccoli brushed with the pesto to the chicken for the last 25 minutes of baking.

➤ **Pesto Tomato Mozzarella Chicken:** Add roasted tomatoes and melted mozzarella cheese to the pesto chicken.

# Simple Sheet Pan Asparagus with Chicken

SEASON:
Spring

This super-simple sheet pan dinner is just what you need on those nights when you don't know what to cook. Serve this over quinoa, rice, or your favorite grain for a quick, healthy, and delicious weeknight meal.

**Serves 4 | Prep time: 5 minutes | Cook time: 25 minutes**

1 pound chicken breasts

3 tablespoons olive oil, divided

2 tablespoons lemon juice

4 garlic cloves, minced

1 teaspoon freshly ground
   black pepper

1 bunch asparagus

1 lemon, zested and sliced

**PER SERVING:** Calories: 303; Total fat: 21g; Carbohydrates: 4g; Fiber: 1g; Protein: 25g; Calcium: 31mg; Vitamin D: 18mcg; Vitamin $B_{12}$: 0mcg; Iron: 2mg; Zinc: 1mg

1. Preheat the oven to 375°F.

2. Put the chicken breasts on a sheet pan, drizzle with 2 tablespoons of olive oil and the lemon juice, and season with the minced garlic and pepper.

3. Bake for 10 minutes, then add the asparagus to the sheet pan, drizzling with the remaining 1 tablespoon of olive oil and sprinkling on the lemon zest. Bake for another 10 to 15 minutes, or until the chicken is cooked to an internal temperature of 165°F.

4. Garnish with thinly sliced lemon and serve.

➤ **Beyond the basics:** Round out this meal by adding roasted potatoes to cook first for 10 minutes and sprinkling with Parmesan cheese.

**VARIATIONS:**

➤ **Sheet Pan Green Beans, Carrots, and Chicken:** Instead of asparagus spears, use green beans and carrots sliced into ½-inch rounds.

➤ **Sheet Pan Summer Squash and Shrimp:** Swap the chicken for shrimp, and use yellow squash and zucchini half-moons for the vegetables, roasting for 10 to 15 minutes total.

# Turkey-Stuffed Zucchini Boats

SEASON:
Summer

Stuffed vegetables are definitely my thing, and these zucchini boats with turkey are as delicious as they are simple to put together. Ground turkey works well with the flavors here, but don't be shy about trying chicken, beef, or tempeh.

**Serves 4 | Prep time: 10 minutes | Cook time: 40 minutes**

4 large zucchini, halved
   lengthwise and seeded

Salt

Freshly ground black pepper

1 tablespoon olive oil

1 onion, chopped small

3 garlic cloves, minced

1 pound ground turkey

1 tablespoon Italian seasoning

3 tablespoons grated
   Parmesan cheese

1 cup Simple Marinara Sauce
   (page 185) or store-bought

1 beefsteak tomato, chopped

1 cup cooked rice

1 cup shredded
   mozzarella cheese

---

**PER SERVING:** Calories: 448;
Total fat: 22g; Carbohydrates: 32g;
Fiber: 5g; Protein: 35g;
Calcium: 272mg; Vitamin D: 21mcg;
Vitamin B$_{12}$: 2mcg; Iron: 4mg;
Zinc: 5mg

1. Preheat the oven to 400°F. Line a sheet pan with parchment paper.

2. Put the zucchini on the sheet pan, scoop-side up. Sprinkle with salt and pepper. Bake for 10 minutes, then remove from the oven and set aside.

3. Heat the olive oil in a large sauté pan or skillet over medium-high heat. Add the onion and sauté until tender and translucent. Add the garlic and cook for 1 more minute, or until fragrant.

4. Add the ground turkey, breaking it up into small pieces with a wooden spoon, and cook until it's thoroughly browned. Drain any excess fat, if needed.

5. Reduce the heat to medium and add the Italian seasoning, Parmesan cheese, marinara sauce, and tomato. Stir to combine, and bring to a gentle simmer.

6. Remove from the heat and stir in the rice.

7. Divide the filling evenly among the zucchini boats. Top each zucchini boat with mozzarella cheese.

8. Bake uncovered for 15 minutes, until the cheese has melted and the zucchini is fork-tender.

**CONTINUED**

# Turkey-Stuffed Zucchini Boats CONTINUED

➤ **Prep tip:** Starting with partially cooked zucchini will ensure that the turkey does not dry out when these boats are baked in the oven again.

## VARIATIONS:

➤ **Southwest Zucchini Boats:** Utilize black beans, corn, and enchilada sauce as a filling, and melt cheddar cheese on top.

➤ **Turkey-Stuffed Acorn Squash:** Sub in winter squash for the zucchini.

# Sheet Pan Sausage, Green Beans, Mushrooms, and Potatoes

SEASON:
Spring, summer, fall, winter

Ready in under 30 minutes using only a few ingredients, this sheet pan dinner is quick, easy, and super satisfying. Plus, you can use this formula to swap out the crispy, browned sausage and tender veggies for whatever you have left in your refrigerator and pantry each week.

**Serves 4 to 6 | Prep time: 5 minutes | Cook time: 25 minutes**

2 pounds small red
   potatoes, halved

2 tablespoons olive oil,
   plus more

Salt

Freshly ground black pepper

1 pound precooked sausage,
   sliced into ¼-inch circles

½ pound fresh green beans

½ pound sliced mushrooms

**PER SERVING:** Calories: 639;
Total fat: 38g; Carbohydrates: 47g;
Fiber: 6g; Protein: 29g;
Calcium: 69mg; Vitamin D: 50mcg;
Vitamin $B_{12}$: 2mcg; Iron: 4mg;
Zinc: 4mg

1. Preheat the oven to 400°F.

2. In a large bowl, drizzle the potatoes with olive oil, and season them with salt and pepper. Transfer the potatoes to a sheet pan and cook for 10 minutes. Add the sausage and cook for another 10 minutes.

3. While the sausage and potatoes are cooking, combine the green beans and mushrooms in the bowl that the potatoes were in, and toss to coat with additional olive oil. On a second sheet pan, combine the green beans and mushrooms, and bake everything for another 5 minutes. Serve hot.

➤ **Prep tip:** If using frozen green beans, let them thaw or rinse them quickly with cold water, then dry them completely before cooking.

**CONTINUED**

## Sheet Pan Sausage, Green Beans, Mushrooms, and Potatoes CONTINUED

**VARIATIONS:**

➢ **Sheet Pan Asparagus, Sweet Potato, and Sausage:**
Replace the green beans with asparagus and the red potatoes with cubed sweet potatoes.

➢ **Grilled Green Beans, Mushrooms, and Potatoes:**
Toss all the veggies with olive oil, salt, and pepper, then transfer them to a grill basket and place it on a grill for 20 to 25 minutes, or until fork-tender. Serve with sausage or your choice of protein.

# Pasta with Peas and Bacon

SEASON:
Spring, summer, fall, winter

VEGETARIAN/
VEGAN OPTION
(see headnote)

This simple take on a traditional Italian dish is ready in under 30 minutes, making it a great option for a midweek meal that the whole family will love. Although the salty bacon and sweet peas are a delicious flavor combo, this dish can be made vegetarian or vegan by using tempeh bacon and nutritional yeast instead of Parmesan.

**Serves 4 to 6 | Prep time: 5 minutes | Cook time: 25 minutes**

¼ pound bacon, chopped (2 or 3 slices)

1 pound small pasta, ditalini or shells

½ cup olive oil, divided

1 medium onion, chopped

1 garlic clove, minced

8 ounces frozen peas

2 teaspoons salt

1 teaspoon freshly ground black pepper

⅓ cup grated Parmesan cheese

**PER SERVING:** Calories: 796; Total fat: 35g; Carbohydrates: 97g; Fiber: 7g; Protein: 23g; Calcium: 118mg; Vitamin D: 2mcg; Vitamin B$_{12}$: 0mcg; Iron: 3mg; Zinc: 3mg

1. Preheat the oven to 400°F. Put the bacon on a sheet pan and bake for 15 to 18 minutes or until crispy.

2. Bring a pot of lightly salted water to a boil. Cook the pasta according to the package directions and desired consistency.

3. While the pasta is cooking, heat 2 tablespoons of olive oil in a pan and add the onion and garlic. Cook until the onion is translucent, 6 to 8 minutes.

4. Add the peas and bacon to the pan and cook, stirring occasionally.

5. When the pasta is cooked, drain and add it to the pan with the onion, garlic, peas, and bacon. Use tongs to toss with the remaining 6 tablespoons of olive oil, season with salt and pepper, and sprinkle with Parmesan to serve.

➤ **Make it easier:** If you have canned peas on hand, they work just as well as fresh or frozen in this recipe.

**CONTINUED**

## Pasta with Peas and Bacon <small>CONTINUED</small>

### VARIATIONS:

➤ **Creamy Carbonara:** In a small bowl, whisk 3 large eggs and set aside. When draining the pasta, reserve 1 cup hot water, adding it to the bowl with eggs. Instead of finishing off the dish with olive oil, add the heated egg mixture and pasta into the pan with the onion, garlic, peas, and bacon. Stir well and allow the sauce to thicken before serving.

➤ **Spaghetti Spinach Parmesan:** Swap ditalini for spaghetti and add 2 cups fresh spinach to the pan when cooking the onion and garlic. Omit the peas or leave them in for extra green goodness.

# Moussaka-Stuffed Eggplant

Traditional moussaka is like a Greek version of lasagna, replacing the pasta layer with fried eggplant slices. This stuffed moussaka uses baked eggplant as a vessel for the savory meat mixture and creamy béchamel sauce. Not a meat-eater? Swap the beef for lentils, and serve this as a stand-alone dish or with a simple side salad.

**SEASON:**
Summer, fall

**VEGETARIAN OPTION**
(see headnote)

**Serves 4 | Prep time: 30 minutes | Cook time: 60 minutes**

2 large eggplants, trimmed and sliced in half lengthwise

1 teaspoon salt

2 tablespoons olive oil

1 teaspoon minced garlic

½ onion, chopped

1 pound ground beef (or lamb)

1 (15-ounce) can diced tomatoes

2 tablespoons butter

2 tablespoons flour

1 cup whole milk

¼ cup grated Parmesan cheese

**PER SERVING:** Calories: 429; Total fat: 23g; Carbohydrates: 28g; Fiber: 11g; Protein: 32g; Calcium: 199mg; Vitamin D: 10mcg; Vitamin B$_{12}$: 3mcg; Iron: 4mg; Zinc: 7mg

1. Score and scoop out some of the eggplant, leaving enough to keep the shape and reserving the scooped insides. Sprinkle both parts of the eggplant with the salt and let it sit for 30 minutes to sweat, then pat it dry with a paper towel.

2. In a large sauté pan or skillet, heat the olive oil and garlic for 2 to 3 minutes, or until aromatic. Add in the onion and sauté until translucent, 10 to 15 minutes. Add in the ground beef and cook until browned, about 10 minutes. Add in the scooped-out eggplant and diced tomatoes, stirring to combine.

3. Fill each eggplant half with a quarter of the beef mixture and transfer the boats to a casserole dish or baking pan.

4. Over medium heat, melt the butter in a sauté pan or skillet, and whisk in the flour until combined. Slowly pour in the milk, whisking constantly until the sauce begins to thicken, about 5 minutes.

**CONTINUED**

## Moussaka-Stuffed Eggplant CONTINUED

5. Top the eggplants with the sauce and sprinkle with Parmesan cheese. Bake for 35 to 40 minutes, or until the top begins to brown.

6. Store the leftovers in the refrigerator for up to 5 days, or freeze for up to 3 months.

➤ **Prep tip:** Before cutting the eggplant in half lengthwise, poke a few holes in the skin to allow steam to escape, and slice off a small piece of skin on either side to allow the eggplant "boat" to lie flat while baking and serving.

### VARIATIONS:

➤ **Stuffed Eggplant Parm:** Skip the ground beef and bechamel sauce, but add in 2 cups of shredded mozzarella cheese and ¼ cup Italian bread crumbs.

➤ **Tex-Mex Stuffed Eggplant:** Fill the eggplants with black beans and corn, topping with shredded cheddar cheese and diced avocado.

# Stuffed Acorn Squash with Beef and Lentils

SEASON:
Fall, winter

Acorn squash acts as a natural bowl for savory beef and lentils, although you could stuff it into other squash or bell peppers. Serve this on top of a wild rice pilaf, or garnish with pumpkin seeds to add some extra texture.

**Serves 4 | Prep time: 15 minutes | Cook time: 45 minutes**

---

2 acorn squash, cut in half lengthwise and scooped

2 tablespoons olive oil

Salt

Freshly ground black pepper

1 tablespoon olive oil

2 garlic cloves, minced

1 yellow onion, diced

½ pound ground beef

½ cup cooked lentils

1 (15-ounce) can diced tomatoes

1 teaspoon chili powder

½ teaspoon ground cumin

---

**PER SERVING:** Calories: 312; Total fat: 14g; Carbohydrates: 35g; Fiber: 8g; Protein: 17g; Calcium: 130mg; Vitamin D: 2mcg; Vitamin B$_{12}$: 1mcg; Iron: 5mg; Zinc: 4mg

1. Preheat the oven to 350°F.

2. Drizzle the insides of the acorn squash with the olive oil and season with salt and pepper. Place them cut-side down in a large baking pan and roast for about 45 minutes.

3. While the squash is cooking, heat the olive oil over medium heat in a sauté pan or skillet, then add in the garlic and onion, and cook until translucent. Add the ground beef and cook until browned, about 10 minutes.

4. Stir in the lentils, tomatoes, chili powder, and cumin.

5. When the squash is finished cooking, scoop in the beef and lentil mixture and serve hot.

➤ **Make it easier:** If your acorn squash is tough to cut into, poke some holes with a fork and microwave it for 1 to 2 minutes before slicing.

---

**VARIATIONS:**

➤ **Stuffed Butternut Squash:** For a slightly sweeter twist, serve this mixture in roasted butternut squash.

➤ **Beef and Lentil Rice Bowl with Roasted Acorn Squash:** Slice the squash into wedges and roast for 20 to 25 minutes, adding it to the top of a bowl with the beef lentil mixture and the cooked rice.

# Cauliflower and Root Vegetable Mash Bowls with Ground Beef

SEASON:
Fall, winter

Think of this dish as a super-simplified shepherd's pie. Garlic and rosemary are a cozy flavor combo for a big bowl of beef and mashed veggies, a well-rounded and inexpensive meal that is sure to satisfy.

**Serves 4 to 6 | Prep time: 5 minutes | Cook time: 25 minutes**

2 tablespoons butter

2 garlic cloves, minced

1 head cauliflower, chopped into florets

1 sweet potato, chopped into ½-inch pieces

1 turnip, peeled and chopped into ½-inch pieces

2 parsnips, peeled and chopped into ½-inch pieces

2 carrots, chopped into ½-inch pieces

1 quart water or vegetable broth

1 tablespoon olive oil

1 pound ground beef

1 teaspoon fresh rosemary, plus more (optional) for garnish

1. In a large pot over medium heat, heat the butter until melted, then add in the garlic and cook for about 2 minutes.

2. Add in the cauliflower, sweet potato, turnip, parsnips, and carrots, stirring well. Pour in the water and bring to a boil. Cook the vegetables for about 20 minutes, or until very tender.

3. While the vegetables are cooking, heat the olive oil in a saucepan and add the ground beef, stirring every 3 to 4 minutes. Add in the rosemary and cook for about 10 minutes, or until fully browned.

4. When the vegetables are soft, drain the remaining liquid and return the vegetables to the pot. Mash them with a potato masher or large spoon, but if a smoother consistency is desired, use an immersion blender or transfer to a large blender.

5. To serve, plate the cooked ground beef and top with mashed vegetables. Garnish with additional rosemary, if desired.

➤ **Beyond the basics:** For a more traditional casserole-style meal, add a small can of diced tomatoes to the beef mixture, and spread it evenly on the bottom of a casserole dish. Top with the mashed veggies and brown in the oven for 10 minutes at 350°F.

## VARIATIONS:

➤ **Red Root Vegetable Mash:** Make a more colorful sweet mash by swapping out parsnips for 1 medium beet.

➤ **Roast Beef and Roasted Root Veggies:** Change this into a sheet pan meal with 1 to 2 pounds beef roast and chopped root vegetables. Preheat the oven to 350°F, season the beef with salt and pepper, and cook for 1 hour 15 minutes or until the beef reaches an internal temperature of 145°, adding the roasted veggies for the last 20 to 30 minutes.

**PER SERVING:** Calories: 367; Total fat: 16g; Carbohydrates: 31g; Fiber: 9g; Protein: 29g; Calcium: 100mg; Vitamin D: 8mcg; Vitamin B$_{12}$: 3mcg; Iron: 4mg; Zinc: 7mg

Cucumber-Radish Salsa, 186

# CHAPTER 8

# Staples, Sauces, and Sweets

# Brussels Sprout Pesto

SEASON:
Late fall to early spring

**VEGETARIAN**

I'm on a serious mission to convince the world how great Brussels sprouts are. They're not only good for digestion and gut health (hello, fiber!), but these little baby cabbages are also packed with vitamin C, vitamin K, potassium, and folate. When properly seasoned and served, as in this simple pesto sauce, Brussels sprouts can be the veggie you didn't know you loved.

**Makes 1½ cups | Prep time: 10 minutes | Cook time: 10 minutes**

⅓ cup pine nuts

2 cups packed Brussels sprout leaves

2 garlic cloves, minced

⅓ cup grated Parmesan cheese

½ cup olive oil

**PER SERVING
(2 TABLESPOONS):** Calories: 123; Total fat: 12g; Carbohydrates: 2g; Fiber: 1g; Protein: 2g; Calcium: 31mg; Vitamin D: 1mcg; Vitamin B$_{12}$: 0mcg; Iron: 0mg; Zinc: 0mg

1. Preheat the oven to 350°F. Spread the pine nuts onto a sheet pan, and place them in the oven to toast, until browned, 8 to 10 minutes. Remove and allow the pine nuts to cool.

2. When the pine nuts are cool, put them in a food processor or blender with the Brussels sprout leaves, garlic, Parmesan, and olive oil. Pulse to combine.

3. Serve with salmon, chicken, or pasta.

➤ **Prep tip:** Do double duty when prepping this recipe. Use leaves for pesto sauce, and roast the rest of the Brussels sprouts to serve as a side dish.

**VARIATIONS:**

➤ **Spinach-Kale Pesto:** Replace the Brussels sprout leaves with 1 cup of spinach and 1 cup of kale leaves for a rich green alternative.

➤ **Broccoli-Basil Pesto:** Give traditional pesto a boost of nutrition by adding ½ cup of broccoli florets to 1½ cups of basil leaves before adding all the remaining ingredients.

# Chimichurri

Similar to a pesto, chimichurri is an herb-filled sauce used most commonly in Argentinian cuisine as a marinade. This veggie version packs in some baby spinach for more color and nutrition and is great on steak, poultry, fish, or even as a dip for bread.

SEASON:
Spring, summer, fall, winter

VEGAN

**Makes about 1 cup | Prep time: 10 minutes**

¾ cup Italian parsley

3 garlic cloves, chopped

2 tablespoons fresh oregano

½ cup baby spinach

⅓ cup olive oil

¼ cup red wine vinegar

2 teaspoons lemon zest

⅛ teaspoon red pepper flakes

Salt

**PER SERVING
(2 TABLESPOONS):** Calories: 85;
Total fat: 9g; Carbohydrates: 1g;
Fiber: 0g; Protein: 0g; Calcium: 17mg;
Vitamin D: 0mcg; Vitamin B$_{12}$: 0mcg;
Iron: 1mg; Zinc: 0mg

1. Combine the parsley, garlic, oregano, and spinach in a food processor. Pulse until the herbs are finely chopped and the garlic is minced.

2. Transfer the herbs to a medium bowl and stir in the olive oil, vinegar, lemon zest, and red pepper flakes. Season with salt to taste.

➤ **Prep tip:** If you don't have a food processor or blender, you can still make this delicious sauce. Just chop the spinach and herbs very finely and mix together in a bowl.

## VARIATIONS:

➤ **Kale Chimichurri:** Replace the baby spinach with kale for a thicker, stronger-tasting sauce.

➤ **Red Pepper Chimichurri:** Add ½ cup chopped red bell pepper instead of baby spinach for a more colorful sauce.

# Green Pea Guacamole

This guac is extra! By now you already know that, but in this case I'm referring to the extra protein it has from green peas. Serve this as a dip for chips or veggie sticks, spread onto a sandwich, or scoop onto your tacos for a unique veggie-filled twist on traditional guacamole.

SEASON:
Spring, summer

VEGAN

**Makes 3½ cups | Prep time: 15 minutes**

1 cup frozen green
   peas, thawed

Juice from 1 lime

4 garlic cloves, minced

3 scallions, both white and
   green parts, roughly chopped

1 teaspoon ground cumin

2 ripe avocados

½ cup fresh cilantro

1 plum tomato, chopped

Salt

Freshly ground black pepper

1. In a food processor, pulse together the green peas, lime juice, garlic, scallions, and cumin until smooth.

2. In a medium bowl, mash the avocado with the back of a fork. Fold in the green pea mixture, cilantro, and tomato.

3. Season with salt and pepper to taste.

4. Serve with tortilla chips or slices of jicama, carrots, or other vegetables of your choice.

➤ **Prep tip:** When choosing avocados, look for a dark green color and gently squeeze. If it feels soft, but not mushy, it's ripe and ready to use.

**PER SERVING (½ CUP):**
Calories: 128; Total fat: 9g; Carbohydrates: 11g; Fiber: 6g; Protein: 3g; Calcium: 26mg; Vitamin D: 0mcg; Vitamin B$_{12}$: 0mcg; Iron: 1mg; Zinc: 1mg

**VARIATIONS:**

➤ **Super Green Guacamole:** Replace peas with kale or spinach for a superfood green guacamole boost.

➤ **Roasted Corn and Black Bean Guacamole:** Instead of peas, add ½ cup of roasted corn and ½ cup of black beans.

# Simple Marinara Sauce

SEASON:
Summer, fall,
winter, spring

**VEGETARIAN**

Making homemade marinara doesn't have to mean sacrificing an entire Sunday. This simple sauce uses canned tomatoes and sauce as a base and adds depth with garlic and herbs. Cook an extra batch each time you make it because it can be stored for 3 to 4 months in the freezer.

**Makes 3 cups | Prep time: 10 minutes | Cook time: 30 minutes**

2 tablespoons olive oil

4 garlic cloves, minced

1 tablespoon tomato paste

1 (28-ounce) can crushed tomatoes

1 (14-ounce) can petite diced tomatoes

1 (8-ounce) can tomato sauce

1 dried bay leaf

2 teaspoons sugar

½ teaspoon salt

1 teaspoon dried basil

¼ teaspoon red pepper flakes

Freshly ground black pepper

**PER SERVING (½ CUP):**
Calories: 121; Total fat: 5g; Carbohydrates: 19g; Fiber: 5g; Protein: 3g; Calcium: 58mg; Vitamin D: 0mcg; Vitamin B$_{12}$: 0mcg; Iron: 3mg; Zinc: 1mg

1. In a large pot, heat the olive oil over medium-high heat. Add the garlic and cook for about 1 minute, or until fragrant. Coat the garlic with tomato paste.

2. Add the crushed tomatoes, diced tomatoes, and tomato sauce.

3. Stir in the bay leaf, sugar, salt, dried basil, and red pepper flakes.

4. Bring to a simmer, uncovered, and continue to simmer for 20 minutes, stirring occasionally.

5. Remove the bay leaf and season with additional salt and black pepper to taste.

➤ **Beyond the basics:** Have some truly fresh summertime tomatoes in your garden? Replace the can of petite diced tomatoes with about 2 cups diced fresh tomatoes for a homegrown *and* homemade sauce.

**VARIATIONS:**

➤ **Mushroom Marinara:** Add 1 cup of chopped fresh mushrooms with crushed tomatoes for a chunkier texture and more umami flavor.

➤ **Root Vegetable Marinara:** Stir in ¼ cup each of chopped carrots, beets, and sweet potato to thicken this sauce.

# Cucumber-Radish Salsa

SEASON:
Spring, summer, fall

**VEGAN**

The sweetness of the cucumber and tomato balances out the spice and bite of the jalapeño for a salsa that is truly rad-ish! Use this salsa on any type of tacos or serve with tortilla chips in place of traditional guac.

**Makes 3½ cups | Prep time: 10 minutes**

½ pound radishes, diced

1 cucumber, diced

½ red onion, diced

1 small jalapeño, diced

1 medium tomato, diced

Juice from 1 lime (about 2 tablespoons)

½ teaspoon salt

¼ teaspoon freshly ground black pepper

Chopped cilantro

**PER SERVING (½ CUP):**
Calories: 20; Total fat: 0g; Carbohydrates: 5g; Fiber: 1g; Protein: 1g; Calcium: 20mg; Vitamin D: 0mcg; Vitamin B$_{12}$: 0mcg; Iron: 0mg; Zinc: 0mg

1. In a mixing bowl, combine the radishes, cucumber, onion, jalapeño, and tomato.

2. Add the lime juice and season with salt and pepper.

3. Add the cilantro to the mixing bowl to taste. Stir until well combined and serve immediately.

➤ **Beyond the basics:** Feeling fancy? Try roasting the radishes, tomatoes, and onion before combining them in a food processor with the cucumber and jalapeño. The resulting salsa won't be as brightly colored, but the flavors will be bold with a combo of soft and crunchy veggies.

**VARIATIONS:**

➤ **Zucchini-Radish Salsa:** Swap the cucumber for zucchini as a way to use up excess summer squash or zucchini.

➤ **Jicama Pico de Gallo:** Ditch the cucumbers and radishes and add 1 jicama, peeled and diced, for a slightly sweeter version of this salsa.

# Romesco Sauce

A tomato-based sauce often used as a dip or served with fish and meats, this romesco comes together quickly using ingredients you probably have in your pantry right now.

SEASON:
Spring, summer, fall, winter

VEGAN

**Makes 3 cups | Prep time: 10 minutes | Cook time: 20 minutes**

2 teaspoons olive oil

4 garlic cloves, minced

2 tablespoon tomato paste

1 teaspoon dried oregano

1 (28-ounce) can diced tomatoes, with juices

½ cup raw walnuts

Salt

Freshly ground black pepper

**PER SERVING (½ CUP):**
Calories: 106; Total fat: 8g; Carbohydrates: 8g; Fiber: 4g; Protein: 3g; Calcium: 61mg; Vitamin D: 0mcg; Vitamin B$_{12}$: 0mcg; Iron: 1mg; Zinc: 1mg

1. In a medium saucepan over medium-low heat, heat the olive oil. Sauté garlic until fragrant, 1 to 2 minutes.

2. Add the tomato paste and stir to coat the garlic. Add the oregano and tomatoes with the juices. Simmer for 20 minutes.

3. Put the walnuts in a food processor and pulse until finely chopped. Add the sauce from the pan to the food processor and pulse until combined with walnuts.

4. Season with salt and pepper to taste.

➤ **Prep tip:** Leftover tomato paste? Line a sheet pan with parchment paper and measure out 1 tablespoonfuls of tomato paste, using up your leftovers. Freeze. Once solid, put the tomato paste in a container and store in the freezer.

**VARIATIONS:**

➤ **Creamy Romesco Sauce:** Create a creamy sauce by stirring in ½ cup of plain yogurt at the end.

➤ **Roasted Red Pepper Romesco:** Replace the tomato paste with 1 large roasted red pepper.

# Homemade Sauerkraut

This fermented food recipe is good for your gut health and also your wallet. For just a few dollars, you can make a probiotic-rich and fiber-filled food that may help improve digestion. Emerging research also shows a strong gut–brain connection and links to immunity, so adding more fermented foods to your diet is probably a good idea, and this homemade 'kraut recipe makes that easy.

**Makes 6 to 8 cups | Prep time: 10 minutes, plus 7 days to ferment**

1 head green cabbage, cored
   and thinly sliced
1 tablespoon salt

**PER SERVING (½ CUP):** Calories: 19;
Total fat: 0g; Carbohydrates: 4g;
Fiber: 2g; Protein: 1g; Calcium: 30mg;
Vitamin D: 0mcg; Vitamin B$_{12}$: 0mcg;
Iron: 0mg; Zinc: 0mg

1. Put the cabbage in a large bowl. Toss with the salt and let stand for 10 minutes. Using a potato masher, press out any excess liquid and set it aside.

2. Spoon the cabbage into a quart-size glass jar and pack down. Add the brine (the excess liquid that was drained from the cabbage) and fill the remaining space with water until the cabbage is fully submerged, leaving at least an inch of space at the top of the jar. Place a small glass jar (like a jelly jar) inside the larger one on top of the cabbage to weigh it down and keep the cabbage fully submerged.

3. Cover the jar with a lid and make sure to open and release the pressure every few days.

4. Store the jar at room temperature for at least 1 week. Taste and continue to ferment until it reaches the desired tanginess. Transfer the jar to the refrigerator to store for up to 6 months.

➤ **Beyond the basics:** After the sauerkraut has been devoured, save the brine and reuse it to get your next batch of fermented veggies going.

**VARIATIONS:**

➤ **Simple Fermented Carrots:** Pour salted water over carrot sticks in a large mason jar. Keep them submerged and follow recipe steps 3 and 4.

➤ **Garlic Sliced Radishes:** Slice radishes and put them in a jar with 2 whole, peeled garlic cloves. Cover with salted water and keep in a closed jar for up to 1 week, releasing the pressure every few days.

# Spicy Beet Ketchup

Let's not beet around the bush: This ketchup is dynamite! Use it on sandwiches, burgers, hot dogs, French fries, and so much more for a spicy kick and boost of folate, vitamin C, and fiber.

**SEASON:**
Summer, fall, winter

**VEGAN**

**Makes 2 cups | Prep time: 5 minutes**

½ pound beets, roasted and cut into chunks

⅓ cup apple cider vinegar

½ teaspoon ground ginger

¼ teaspoon salt

⅛ teaspoon freshly ground black pepper

¼ cup brown sugar (ensure vegan, if needed)

**PER SERVING
(2 TABLESPOONS):** Calories: 20; Total fat: 0g; Carbohydrates: 5g; Fiber: 0g; Protein: 0g; Calcium: 6mg; Vitamin D: 0mcg; Vitamin B$_{12}$: 0mcg; Iron: 0mg; Zinc: 0mg

1. In a food processor, combine the beet chunks, vinegar, ginger, salt, pepper, and brown sugar.

2. Pulse until well combined. Use immediately or store in the refrigerator for up to 3 weeks.

➤ **Make it easier:** Look for vacuum-packed cooked beets at the grocery store to save time and effort.

**VARIATIONS:**

➤ **Roasted Vegetable Ketchup:** Swap the beets for 1 cup of roasted carrots, ½ cup of roasted butternut squash, and 6 ounces of canned tomato paste. Add water as needed while pulsing to produce a smooth consistency.

➤ **Beet Yogurt Dip:** Add ½ cup plain yogurt to the mix for a creamy dip or spread.

# Tzatziki

The sweetness of the cucumber offsets the tartness of the yogurt and tang of garlic in just the right amounts. Dollop onto souvlaki platters; use as a dip for fresh pita bread; or, if you're like me, enjoy this tzatziki sauce on its own by the spoonful.

SEASON:
Summer

VEGETARIAN

**Makes 2½ cups | Prep time: 40 minutes**

1 English cucumber
1½ teaspoons salt, divided
2 cups plain Greek yogurt
1 garlic clove, grated
1 lemon, zested and juiced
1 tablespoon chopped
  fresh dill
1 tablespoon olive oil
Freshly ground black pepper

**PER SERVING (¼ CUP):**
Calories: 50; Total fat: 3g;
Carbohydrates: 4g; Fiber: 0g;
Protein: 2g; Calcium: 75mg;
Vitamin D: 1mcg; Vitamin B$_{12}$: 0mcg;
Iron: 0mg; Zinc: 0mg

1. Slice the cucumber lengthwise, scrape out with a spoon, and dice the remaining cucumber. Put the cucumbers in a mesh strainer and sprinkle with 1 teaspoon of salt. Stir to combine. Let sit and drain for 30 minutes to 1 hour. Using a thin cloth or paper towel, blot any excess moisture from the cucumbers.

2. In a medium bowl, combine the cucumber, Greek yogurt, garlic, lemon zest, lemon juice, dill, the remaining ½ teaspoon of salt, and the olive oil. Stir until well combined. Season with pepper to taste.

➤ **Beyond the basics:** If time allows, let tzatziki sauce sit in the refrigerator for a few hours before serving to allow the flavors to meld together.

**VARIATIONS:**

➤ **Radish Tzatziki:** Replace cucumber with ½ cup of finely chopped radishes.
➤ **Red Beet Tzatziki:** Stir 1 cup roasted, shredded red beet into the Greek yogurt mixture instead of (or in addition to) the cucumber.

# Beet Brownie Skillet

I know what you're thinking . . . vegetable brownies? But hear me out before you pass on this unbeet-able dessert. Roasted beets with creamy yogurt produces a natural sweetness, rich color, and more depth of flavor. If you don't want to tell anyone there are veggies in this skillet, the secret is safe with me.

**SEASON:**
Spring, summer, fall, winter

**VEGETARIAN**

**Makes 12 brownies | Prep time: 20 minutes | Cook time: 1 hour, 50 minutes**

## FOR THE BEET PUREE
1 beet
⅓ cup plain yogurt

## FOR THE BROWNIES
½ cup unsalted butter, melted
1 cup sugar
¾ cup unsweetened
    cocoa powder
½ teaspoon salt
2 large eggs
2 teaspoons vanilla extract
1 cup beet puree
¾ cup all-purpose flour
½ teaspoon baking powder
⅔ cup chocolate chips

**PER SERVING:** Calories: 258; Total fat: 13g; Carbohydrates: 34g; Fiber: 3g; Protein: 4g; Calcium: 41mg; Vitamin D: 13mcg; Vitamin B$_{12}$: 0mcg; Iron: 2mg; Zinc: 1mg

1. **To make the beet puree:** Preheat the oven to 400°F. Remove the stem from the beet and scrub the skin under cold water. Wrap the beet in aluminum foil and place in the oven. Cook for about 1 hour, or until it's fork-tender.

2. Open the foil and let the beet cool for a few minutes, until it can be handled, then peel away the skin.

3. In a food processor, puree the beet and yogurt until very smooth. Set aside.

4. **To make the brownies:** Preheat the oven to 325°F. Spray an 8- or 10-inch cast-iron skillet with cooking spray.

5. In a large bowl, combine the melted butter, sugar, cocoa powder, and salt.

6. In a separate bowl, beat the eggs. Pour them into the butter mixture and stir until well combined. Add the vanilla extract and beet puree, mixing well.

7. Stir in the flour ¼ cup at a time, and mix in the baking powder until just combined.

8. Fold in the chocolate chips. Pour the mixture evenly into the greased skillet.

9. Bake for 45 to 50 minutes, or until a toothpick inserted comes out clean.

➢ **Make it easier:** Don't have time to roast beets? No problem—use canned beets.

## VARIATIONS:

➢ **Sweet Potato Brownies:** Swap out beets for steamed sweet potatoes and follow the recipe as is.

➢ **Zucchini Brownies:** Instead of beets, mix 1 cup of shredded zucchini with yogurt. Puree only if you're really trying to hide the veggies.

# Carrot-Mango Sorbet

SEASON:
Summer

VEGAN

Enjoy this frozen treat for a boost of vitamins A and C, which can contribute to immunity, bone and eye health, and more. The vodka isn't to make the sorbet boozy, but rather to help the mixture from freezing completely solid. If you prefer to omit the vodka, just remove the sorbet from the freezer to soften about 15 minutes before serving.

**Serves 8 | Prep time: 15 minutes, plus 4 hours freezing time**

2 cups chopped and
  steamed carrots

2 ripe mangos, chopped

2 cups water

1 cup sugar

Juice of ½ orange

2 tablespoons vodka (optional)

**PER SERVING:** Calories: 163; Total fat: 0g; Carbohydrates: 41g; Fiber: 3g; Protein: 1g; Calcium: 22mg; Vitamin D: 0mcg; Vitamin $B_{12}$: 0mcg; Iron: 0mg; Zinc: 0mg

1. In a blender, combine the steamed carrots, mangos, water, sugar, orange juice, and vodka, if using. Blend until smooth.

2. Pour into a freezer-safe container and let freeze for at least 4 hours. For a creamier consistency, every 30 minutes or so, remove the sorbet from the freezer and use a fork to break up the mixture and smash chunks of sorbet. Smooth out and return the sorbet to the freezer until completely frozen.

➤ **Make it easier:** Instead of fresh, use frozen mango and frozen carrots, steamed quickly in the microwave.

**VARIATIONS:**

➤ **Beet-Berry Sorbet:** Replace the carrots with 2 cups cooked beets and the mango with about 3 cups of berries.

➤ **Cucumber Mojito Sorbet:** Leave out the mango and swap in 3 medium cucumbers for the carrots. Replace the orange juice with lime juice and add fresh mint leaves or ¼ teaspoon of dried (a little goes a long way).

# Cinnamon Jicama Chips

SEASON:
Fall, winter, spring

**VEGETARIAN,
VEGAN OPTION**

Jicama is a root vegetable, so it makes sense that it could be turned into a yummy chip. These are crispy and sweet all on their own, but they can also be served with a fruit and yogurt dip, or even chocolate.

**Serves 2 to 4 | Prep time: 5 minutes | Cook time: 20 minutes**

2 jicama, peeled and halved

1 tablespoon olive oil

2 teaspoons ground cinnamon

1 teaspoon light brown
  sugar, ensure vegan,
  if needed (optional)

**PER SERVING:** Calories: 325;
Total fat: 7g; Carbohydrates: 62g;
Fiber: 34g; Protein: 5g;
Calcium: 107mg; Vitamin D: 0mcg;
Vitamin B$_{12}$: 0mcg; Iron: 4mg;
Zinc: 1mg

1. Preheat the oven to 400°F. Line a sheet pan with parchment paper.

2. Thinly slice the jicama using a sharp knife or a mandoline, and spread the slices evenly on a sheet pan.

3. Lightly brush the jicama chips with olive oil, then sprinkle with cinnamon and brown sugar, if using.

4. Bake for 15 to 20 minutes, flipping halfway.

➤ **Prep tip:** You may need to cook these a few minutes less or a few minutes more depending on your stove and the thickness of the chip slices. Place the sheet pan on the middle rack of the oven for consistency.

**VARIATIONS:**

➤ **Sweet Potato Chips:** For a sweet and salty veggie chip, follow this recipe but replace the jicama with sweet potato, sprinkling with a little sea salt instead of cinnamon and sugar.

➤ **Jicama Churros:** Rather than thin slices, cut the jicama in half lengthwise and then chop it into sticks, or purchase prepared jicama sticks. Coat with oil, cinnamon, and sugar, and bake as directed above or panfry.

# Pumpkin, Fig, and Apple Crisp

SEASON:
Fall

**VEGETARIAN**

Adapted from my mom's apple crisp recipe, this is a delicious way to take us from summer to fall with the pumpkin, fig, apple, and cinnamon flavors. Each serving has about 9 grams of fiber, and while my favorite way to serve this is warm right out of the oven, with a scoop of vanilla ice cream on top, you can also enjoy it for breakfast, with some savory eggs on the side.

**Serves 6 | Prep time: 20 minutes | Cook time: 45 minutes**

6 medium apples, sliced

1 cup pumpkin puree

6 figs, quartered

1 tablespoon ground cinnamon, plus more

½ cup plus 1 teaspoon sugar, divided

2 tablespoons butter

2 eggs

1½ cups whole-wheat flour

1 teaspoon baking powder

**PER SERVING:** Calories: 388; Total fat: 6g; Carbohydrates: 81g; Fiber: 9g; Protein: 7g; Calcium: 103mg; Vitamin D: 17mcg; Vitamin B$_{12}$: 0mcg; Iron: 3mg; Zinc: 1mg

1. Preheat the oven to 350°F.

2. In a large bowl, using a wooden spoon, stir together the sliced apples, pumpkin, figs, 1 tablespoon of cinnamon, and 1 teaspoon of sugar until the apples and figs are evenly coated.

3. Transfer the fruit mixture to a 9-by-13-inch baking pan. Cut the butter into small cubes and place them evenly on top of the fruit.

4. In a separate bowl, beat the eggs with the remaining ½ cup of sugar. Add the flour, baking powder, and a sprinkle of cinnamon. Stir until a sticky dough is formed.

5. Using your hands, crumble the dough in clumps over the top of the fruit.

6. Bake 45 minutes, or until the crumble is browned.

**CONTINUED**

# Pumpkin, Fig, and Apple Crisp

➤ **Prep tip:** If you find yourself with leftovers (though doubtful), or if you make this dish in advance, try not to cover it so the crumble topping stays crispy. Reheat for a few minutes under a broiler to crisp up the topping again.

## VARIATIONS:

➤ **Butternut Squash and Apple Crisp:** Replace the pumpkin puree with 1 cup of roasted and mashed butternut squash.

➤ **Pumpkin-Zucchini Crisp:** Swap out the apples for 2 large peeled zucchini. Cut each in half lengthwise, salt for 5 to 10 minutes, pat dry, then slice and follow directions as written.

# Sweet Corn Ice Cream

SEASON:
Summer

VEGETARIAN

The summer I first tried sweet corn ice cream at a local farm stand, my world was changed. If you have an ice cream maker hidden away in a cabinet somewhere, it's time to bust it out and get the freezer bowl ready for some veggie ice cream. For the record, this recipe is less about finding a way to sneak vegetables into your dessert and more about celebrating the delicious flavors that sweet corn brings to us each summer—in a creamy, frozen treat. Don't have an ice cream maker? No problem. See the tip.

**Serves: 8 to 10 | Prep time: 5 minutes | Cook time: 15 minutes, plus 40 minutes to freeze**

3 cups sweet corn, approximately 2 (15-ounce) cans or 3 or 4 ears fresh corn

2 cups heavy cream

1 cup whole milk

1 tablespoon vanilla extract

1 cup sugar

4 egg yolks

**PER SERVING:** Calories: 358; Total fat: 23g; Carbohydrates: 35g; Fiber: 1g; Protein: 5g; Calcium: 76mg; Vitamin D: 31mcg; Vitamin $B_{12}$: 0mcg; Iron: 1mg; Zinc: 1mg

1. Turn the oven to broil. If taking the kernels off the cob, lay flat and slice one side completely off to create a stable base to remove the rest. Spread the corn kernels evenly on a sheet pan and place under the broiler until they begin to brown, about 5 minutes.

2. In a saucepan, heat the heavy cream, milk, corn, and vanilla extract on medium heat. Bring to a simmer, but do not boil, about 5 minutes. If a smoother consistency is desired, use an immersion blender to puree some of the corn kernels.

3. While heating the cream mixture, whisk together the sugar and egg yolks.

4. Slowly add the hot cream mixture to the bowl with the eggs and sugar, stirring constantly.

5. Chill in the refrigerator for 15 minutes.

**CONTINUED**

6. Pour the ice cream base into an ice cream maker, turn on, and churn according to the manufacturer's instructions, approximately 25 minutes.

7. Serve immediately or cover with plastic wrap and keep in the freezer.

➤ **Beyond the basics:** Make this ice cream even if you don't have an ice cream maker. Simply transfer the cooled ice cream base to a stainless steel dish or bowl, then move it to the freezer for 45 minutes. Check the ice cream and stir vigorously every 45 minutes for 6 hours, or until the ice cream is evenly frozen.

## VARIATIONS:

➤ **Cucumber Ice Cream:** Instead of roasted corn, de-seed and shred 2 cucumbers to add to the cream mixture. Transfer the ice cream base to a blender to puree before pouring it into the ice cream maker.

➤ **Sweet Potato Ice Cream:** Replace the corn with 1½ cups mashed sweet potato and 1 tablespoon ground cinnamon.

# Zucchini Bread Cookies

SEASON:
Summer

VEGETARIAN

Toward the end of each summer, thanks to our beautiful backyard garden, I find myself up to my ears in zucchini. These soft and chewy zucchini cookies came about as a way to put that zucchini to work. They can and should be enjoyed for breakfast, dessert, or a snack any time of day. Plus, the cleanup is quick because these are made in just one bowl, so these veggie treats are sure to please kids and adults alike.

**Makes 24 cookies | Prep time: 10 minutes | Cook time: 15 minutes**

---

3 large eggs

⅓ cup maple syrup

1 tablespoon vanilla extract

½ cup unsalted butter, melted

½ cup shredded zucchini

1½ cups old-fashioned oats

1½ cups whole-wheat flour

1 teaspoon cinnamon

½ teaspoon ground ginger

½ teaspoon ground nutmeg

1 teaspoon baking soda

¼ cup pecans, crushed

---

**PER SERVING:** Calories: 128; Total fat: 6g; Carbohydrates: 15g; Fiber: 2g; Protein: 4g; Calcium: 19mg; Vitamin D: 8mcg; Vitamin B12: 0mcg; Iron: 1mg; Zinc: 1mg

1. Preheat the oven to 350°F. Line 2 sheet pans with parchment paper and set aside.

2. In a large mixing bowl, whisk together the eggs, syrup, vanilla, and butter. Add in the shredded zucchini to coat, then push the wet ingredients to one side of the bowl.

3. Add the oats, flour, cinnamon, ginger, nutmeg, and baking soda to the other side of the bowl, then stir the wet and dry to combine.

4. Once mixed, add crushed pecans. Drop rounded tablespoons of the dough on the prepared sheet pans, spacing them about an inch apart, and bake for 15 to 18 minutes.

➤ **Prep tip:** Have an abundance of zucchini or squash on hand? Grate it, squeeze out the excess moisture, and freeze to use for baked goods year-round.

---

**VARIATIONS:**

➤ **Carrot Cake Cookies:** Swap the grated zucchini for shredded carrots and bake for 12 to 15 minutes.

➤ **Sweet Potato Cookies:** Use mashed sweet potato to replace the zucchini, and cut the flour by ½ cup.

# Seasonal Vegetable Chart

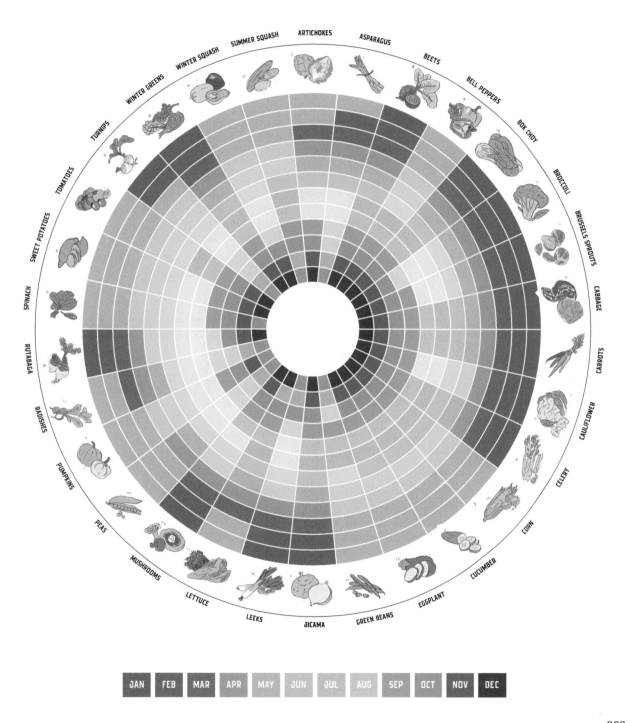

# Measurement Conversions

## VOLUME EQUIVALENTS (LIQUID)

| US Standard | US Standard (ounces) | Metric (approximate) |
|---|---|---|
| 2 tablespoons | 1 fl. oz. | 30mL |
| ¼ cup | 2 fl. oz. | 60mL |
| ½ cup | 4 fl. oz. | 120mL |
| 1 cup | 8 fl. oz. | 240mL |
| 1½ cups | 12 fl. oz. | 355mL |
| 2 cups or 1 pint | 16 fl. oz. | 475mL |
| 4 cups or 1 quart | 32 fl. oz. | 1L |
| 1 gallon | 128 fl. oz. | 4L |

## OVEN TEMPERATURES

| Fahrenheit (F) | Celsius (C) (approximate) |
|---|---|
| 250°F | 120°C |
| 300°F | 150°C |
| 325°F | 165°C |
| 350°F | 180°C |
| 375°F | 190°C |
| 400°F | 200°C |
| 425°F | 220°C |
| 450°F | 230°C |

## VOLUME EQUIVALENTS (DRY)

| US Standard | Metric (approximate) |
|---|---|
| ⅛ teaspoon | 0.5mL |
| ¼ teaspoon | 1mL |
| ½ teaspoon | 2mL |
| ¾ teaspoon | 4mL |
| 1 teaspoon | 5mL |
| 1 tablespoon | 15mL |
| ¼ cup | 59mL |
| ⅓ cup | 79mL |
| ½ cup | 118mL |
| ⅔ cup | 156mL |
| ¾ cup | 177mL |
| 1 cup | 235 mL |
| 2 cups or 1 pint | 475mL |
| 3 cups | 700mL |
| 4 cups or 1 quart | 1L |

## WEIGHT EQUIVALENTS

| US Standard | Metric (approximate) |
|---|---|
| ½ ounce | 15g |
| 1 ounce | 30g |
| 2 ounces | 60g |
| 4 ounces | 115g |
| 8 ounces | 225g |
| 12 ounces | 340g |
| 16 ounces or 1 pound | 455g |

# Index

# Acknowledgments

This book would not be possible without the incredible team at Callisto Media. Thank you for holding my hand through the writing process and always appreciating my vegetable puns.

Special thanks to Julie, for your culinary wisdom and skills, and your endless creativity in the kitchen.

To my biggest cheerleader and lifelong friend Steph, thank you for testing so many of these recipes. 'Preciate you.

To my parents, for showing me what hard work looks like and teaching me that if I can dream it, I can do it.

And last but certainly not least, I express my endless gratitude to Mike, my forever taste tester, and to my son, Easton, the greatest joy I have ever known. I'm not sure all the recipes in this cookbook could keep up with the appetites you boys have, but I look forward to trying to keep your bellies full and your taste buds happy for the rest of my life. I love you both beyond words.

# About the Author

**Kim Hoban** is a registered dietitian, certified intuitive eating counselor, and NASM-certified personal trainer with a passion for food and helping people make peace with their bodies. Brussels sprouts are Kim's favorite vegetable, and when she's not cooking up new veggie recipes, you can find Kim practicing yoga, exploring a new hiking trail, or procrasti-baking. Kim lives on Long Island, New York, with her fiancé, Mike, their son, Easton, and two rescue pit bulls.